T0064461

Development
and Its
Diverse
Aspects

Development
and Its
Diverse
Aspects

Jamil Farooqui
Ahmad A Nasr

PARTRIDGE
A Penguin Random House Company

To order additional copies of this book, contact
Toll Free 800 101 2657 (Singapore)
Toll Free 1 800 81 7340 (Malaysia)
orders.singapore@partridgepublishing.com

www.partridgepublishing.com/singapore

CONTENTS

Introduction..vii

Chapter I 1
    Development And Ummatic Vision: An Overview
        Mohamed Aris Othman
Chapter II 12
    Islamic Perspective Of Development
        Jamil Farooqui
Chapter III.. 43
    Frogs Under a Coconut Shell or Under a Glass Bowl?
    Print Media, Peninsular Orang Asli and Development
        Ahmad A. Nasr
Chapter IV.. 86
    The Importance Of Self-Realization In Human And
      Societal
    Development According To Muhammad Iqbal
    (1877-1938)
        Adibah binti Abdul Rahim
Chapter V 105
    Worldview And Human Development In Secular And
    Islamic Framework
        Hafas Furqani
        & Zakariya Bin Man

Chapter VI..128

    An Islamic Perspective On Consumption, Saving
       And Investment:

    To Flourish A Barakah Wealth Of Ummah

       Dayangku Aslinah Abd. Rahim

Chapter VII 149

    The Development Of Waqf Institution In Malaysia:

    A Study From Historical And Contemporary
       Perspectives

       A Rahman Tang Abdullah

Chapter VIII..162

    The Role Of Grameen Bank In The Social
    Development Of Bangladesh

       Md. Sayed Uddin

End Notes...187

INTRODUCTION

Development is the agenda and the priority of almost all nations. They try to provide their people with a better way of living and better life-chances. In this attempt, they concentrate on the economic and political systems of their societies and try to improve them to achieve the target. The general feeling is that if one increases national wealth, raises physical quality of life and gives freedom to the populace to govern themselves, one achieves prosperity. The past three centuries have shown that nations have made tremendous efforts to boost their economic productions and refine the governing systems. They initiated industrialization, increased capital formation and developed sophisticated technology to change the physical conditions of their societies. They further democratized their socio-economic and political institutions to create a conducive atmosphere for development. Some claimed that they had achieved the level of development, others were in the process and still others have failed to do so. The reality is that the so-called development has failed to provide peaceful, harmonious, contended and dignified life to humans. Still the majority of the people have no sufficient means to live with dignity and honour, they are living below poverty line, are exploited, suppressed and subjugated by those who are wealthy, affluent and enjoying power. Development as generally perceived, by and large, brings luck to small portion of the population who no doubt have all the amenities of life, live luxuriously and enjoy all the privileges of society but the rest of the population are deprived of basic requirements of life. *The Human Development Report 1992* reported that the rich have grown richer and the poor have become poorer due to the outcome of universal development efforts.

The Third World has also initiated the process of development and as such it followed the footstep of the West to change the people. The Third World has however, failed to achieve the satisfactory level of development and has instead damaged its basic values for which it was characterized. The reason is that it did not adopt the Western pattern as such but accommodated it within its own socio-cultural ethos. The result is that developmental efforts could not bring about the same result as it did in the Western soil. Moreover, the Western model of development is not suited to the intellectual and social scenario of these countries; thereby, it created contradiction instead of delivering good.

The problem is that development has not been taken in its true spirit. It has been misunderstood and generally only related to economic development, particularly to Per Capita Income, Gross National Product (GNP) and Physical Quality of Life Index (PQLI) according to which the prosperity of a nation is measured. In fact, development is a comprehensive term; it relates to the overall well-being of individuals and society as well. It refers to integrated human development where humans satisfy their material needs in a dignified way and with basic moral and ethical standards. Material development and the acquisition of wealth are not bad, but they should be within the framework of the right principles (*haq*) and justice (*'adl*), not the other way around. This is what Islam teaches in the context of the development of individuals and societies. The Qur'an categorically says:

> Do not acquire wealth from each other wrongfully, nor knowingly, offer it to authorities with the

objective of unjustly acquiring the wealth of others (Qur'an, 2: 188).

The Qur'an, further, instructs human beings to acquire wealth and meet the requirements of life with decorum through appropriate and just ways and not through mischief.

> And seek, with the wealth that God has given you, the abode of the Hereafter, but do not forget your share in this world. And do good (to others) as God has done to you, and spread not mischief, for God does not like those who do mischief (Qur'an, 28: 77).

Development in Islam is a broad term referring to the improvement of human life in all of its dimensions, including spiritual, moral and material. It is also not limited to one section or group of society, but it is related to the well-being of all human beings. Similarly, it is not only concerned with the prosperity and development of human beings in this world but also assures their welfare in life in the hereafter. Islam is a system of life based on high ideals and virtues and thus requires humans to be equipped with high moral qualities to run the system. For this purpose, it always tries to refine human qualities, improve human potentialities and polish human behaviour so that they may emerge as true servants of God who can establish His system on earth, carry the torch of righteousness in every corners of the world and take care of their fellow beings, society and the entire humanity.

Development is collective action to improve the environment and life conditions so that humans can live in peace and harmony, treat others as their kith and kin and help them to lead a dignified life. It establishes an altruistic society, a just social order where humans get full opportunity to develop their potentialities, utilize resources that God has bestowed upon them, share them equitably with their fellow members and promote truth, justice and rightness. Ahmad (2000: 19) describes the purpose of development in Islam as follows:

The developmental effort, in an Islamic framework, is directed towards the development

> of a God-conscious human being, balanced personality committed to and capable of acting as the witness of truth to mankind and towards establishing a society that is just, growing and capable of meeting the real needs of man and society without exploiting other and encroaching their rights.

Development is thus, "a goal-oriented and value-realizing activity, involving the active participation of man and directed towards the maximization of human well-being in all of its aspects" (Ahmad, ibid.). It requires a distinct psyche, a bent of mind to think how we have to live in this world and meet life conditions in appropriate and dignified ways. If we follow the path of truth, rightness and justice, we get prosperity and success, live our lives peacefully and also let others live in the same way. If we concentrate only on material well-being and try to achieve it, by hook or by crook, through indulgence in wrong-doing and deviation from the truth, we will be led to chaos and destruction. In this attempt, we will not hesitate to take the privileges of others and deprive them of their genuine right of existence.

Life condition does not mean only to satisfy humans' needs and urges to the best possible way but it, in fact, entails how and for what human needs have to be satisfied. It demands that we should think of the purpose of life and direct our operation in this world to realize that purpose. Satisfaction of human needs is the means, not an end. It should be done to achieve the vital and noble purpose for which we are created and given the responsibility of setting up the sovereignty and suzerainty of God in all aspects of our lives and on earth as well. If we accomplish this mission, we will make this world worth living and set up a society where humans could live in peace and harmony, help each other in strengthening righteousness, truth and justice and avoiding falsehood, wrong-doing and injustice.

Modern humans are highly exposed to the pomp and show of material progress that provides glamour to life and make astonishing addition to it day by day. Most individuals want to achieve some level of that progress as well as some part of that glamour in their lives to be conversant with the traits of material life and to equate with their fellow members. They struggle hard and get so much involved in material gain that they neglect the right path to achieve it and adopt any means to acquire it. The result is that they want to grab all the privileges and do not share with others. They do not hesitate even to destroy the natural environment, deprive others of their right of existence and suppress the poor and the downtrodden to get more and more. Sometimes they rationalize their act by developing certain theoretical frameworks and catchy terms to soothe the common man and hide the detrimental consequences of the material progress.

The present book deals with the concept of development and the efforts made to achieve some levels of it in various aspects of our lives. It explains diverse aspects of development which we witness in our society. It consists of ten articles which were presented at the Conference on Development organized by the Department of Sociology and Anthropology, International Islamic University Malaysia. It is of great interest and help for students to know how the process of change is initiated and has modified different aspects of human life.

The first chapter, 'Development and Ummatic Vision: An Overview' underlines that development in the Muslim world can take place in a better and meaningful way through the Islamic concept of *ukhwah* or Muslim brotherhood. Aris Othman explains that Muslims are characterized by their distinct ideology that links them into one cohesive group and transcends all other links and associations. If we activate and revitalize this concept, we can develop unity among Muslim countries and join hands to change the conditions of Muslims worldwide. We can do this through Islamic organizations like the World Muslim Congress (*Mo'tamar al-Islami*) and OIC (Organization of Islamic Countries). They can play a vital role in bringing Muslim countries together, promoting Islamic solidarity and making concentrated efforts to develop the countries. There are 57 members of OIC; the countries have plenty of natural resources and potentials. If they can make systematic and planned efforts, they can not only alleviate poverty but also achieve overall development of their respective countries. Arith Othman identifies seven factors that adversely affect the development of Muslim countries. He further suggests certain measures to remove the preset impediments.

Jamil Farooqui in 'Islamic Perspective of Development: An Alternative Approach' discusses different approaches to development and emphasizes that the term is generally used in a limited sense, relating to economic and political development. He explains that development is a comprehensive term and encompasses all aspects of human life and society, including ideological and material. The best term that connotes, according to him, the correct notion of development is 'social transformation' used by classical sociologists. Islam also stresses on total human development that is the development in all dimensions of human life and society. It is the perfection of human life and as such, changes in all other aspects should be in the context of moral and ideological development. The important aspect of the paper is the rejection of the contemporary view that changes in material conditions initiate changes in the ideological system, including standards of morality, values and virtues. All these norms should be moulded according to the traits of material development. Jamil Farooqui repudiates this view and highlights its repercussions. He explains that if we allow material conditions to change ideological bases, it will destroy the whole fabric of human relations creating conflict, violence, suppression, exploitation, and will damage peace, tranquility and human dignity. He sets forth the Islamic view that changes and development of material conditions should take place according to the ideological bases and cardinal principles of society. This is, in fact, the basis of development in an Islamic perspective where changes first take place in the intellectual set-up and then in material conditions that become more meaningful and beneficial.

Ahmad A. Nasr in his article 'Frogs Under a Coconut Shell or Under a Glass Bowl? Print Media, Peninsular Orang Asli and Development' examines the process of development among Orang Asli (the indigenous people of Peninsular Malaysia). He has based his analysis on the portrayal of development in the print media, particularly in the *New Straits Times* (NST) between the years 2005 - 2009. He has also made occasional references to earlier issues of the paper as well as other Malay newspapers such as *Kosmo, Haritan Metro, Utusan Malaysia* and *Berita Harian*. He has also taken into consideration Mustafa K. Anwar's preliminary study on the presentation of minorities based on the content of the print media in two English newspapers (NST and The Star) in August 1993 and April 1994. Ahmad A. Nasr finds the presentation valid, to some extent, though the period of observation was short. Moreover, he also examines the contents related to Orang Asli and their development as reflected in the efforts of JHEOA and observes that Orang Asli are not against development as they are projected in the print media, but want development in line with their culture.

Adibah binti Abdul Rahim discusses the importance of self-realization in human and societal development. She applies Iqbal's concept of *Khudi* (selfhood) to the revitalization of the system of life and creation of sound and potential personalities among Muslims. She observes the drawbacks of Muslims in their conservative attitudes of self-negation and self-abandonment that make them inactive. They consider active involvement in the world something bad; as such they do not take much interest in the world and prefer to keep themselves aloof from worldly affairs. This is against the spirit of Islam, which encourages participation in the affairs of the universe so that it may be reformed and made worth living. Adibah discusses Iqbal's concept of self, the activation of which creates capable and potential humans who can better play the role of vicegerents of God on earth. She explains that self-realization not only develops human qualities, but it also establishes a close link between individuals and society as it creates conducive condition to develop the self. Thus, self-assertion and self-realization can play an important role in the development of humans and society as well.

Hafas Furqani and Zakariya Man explain the importance of worldview in influencing human thought and action as well as his entire life. They trace the impact of worldview on change, progress and development, giving the example of two systems of thought: secular and Islamic. They compare both systems to solve the economic problems of human beings. The secular worldview stresses on human efforts to satisfy economic needs on the basis of high utility and satisfaction and develops the concept of 'homo-ecnomicus' or economic man. The Islamic worldview based on Divine revelation takes into account the moral standards and societal needs in the satisfaction of human economic needs and sets forth the concept of 'Islamic man'.

Dayangku Aslinah Abd. Rahim discusses the economic system and its three major components: consumption, saving and investment from an Islamic perspective. She observes that if these ingredients are performed according to the Islamic principles, it will be easier to achieve prosperity and remove poverty. Muslims have adequate potentiality and equipped with both physical and spiritual strength to search the bounties of God. If they use and utilize the natural and social resources properly, they will have enough earnings and solve the economic problems of society. She suggests that the production, consumption and distribution of resources should be done according to the principles and provisions of the Qur'an and *Sunnah* in order to boost the economy. This will solve the economic problems of society while at the same time get reward from God.

A. Rahman Tang Abdullah traces the origin and evolution of Waqf as a religious institution in Malaysia. He explains its historical roots and points out the changes that took place in the late twentieth and early twenty-first centuries. The institution of Waqf in Malaysia, according to him, is a dynamic institution as it has developed new features and emerged as an effective mechanism to provide benefits to needy people. The important feature of Waqf in Malaysia is the corporatization of its structure as well as its expansion as a commercial and charitable institution. Moreover, it has also established cash Waqf thus, distinguishing it from other Waqf institutions and making it a distinct one. The author also explores how the present structure of Waqf in Malaysia corroborates or differentiates from the original nature and function of Waqf as embodied in Islamic religious writings. Any conflicting issue arising out of the study should be taken into consideration by men of knowledge in view of the principle of *Istibdal*.

Md. Sayed Uddin discusses the role of Grameen (rural) Bank, a significant Non-Government Organization (NGO) in eradicating poverty of rural people of Bangladesh. It is proved an effective way to change the fate of people by making them rely on their own efforts rather than on the help of others. It injects new zeal among the people and creates initiative among them to start their own businesses and subsequently change their socio-economic condition. The bank introduces a scheme to give credit to rural people to start business, earn money and repay the credit gradually in due course. The people take much interest, work hard and become economically productive. The scheme brings about tremendous change in the lives of people, particularly among rural women who are now more confident and have the potential to initiate economic activities and earn money. The result is that the family life of the people is quite improved in comparison to the past. The author highlights that Grameen Bank negates the view that women are not good entrepreneurs; they cannot perform economic activities well and as such cannot repay t loans. The fact is that the Bank empowered women to stand on their own feet.

The above articles are the few manifestations of developmental activities in various societies. It indicates the nature of human efforts to change the different aspects of society. It further helps us to understand the process of change in developing societies; how we can improve the speed of these changes and make them more effective and meaningful.

Jamil Farooqui
International Islamic University Malaysia

END NOTE

Ahmad, Khurshid, 'Islamic Approach to Development', in *Political Development An Islamic Perspective* ed. Zeenath Kausar (The Other Press in association with the Research Centre, International Islamic University Malysia,2000), 19.

DEVELOPMENT AND UMMATIC VISION: AN OVERVIEW

Mohamed Aris Othman

The focus of this paper is on the development of the *ummah* to face the challenges of the new millennium. This entails development launched from all dimensions by existing agencies in the Muslim world especially those under the umbrella of OIC.

A very important pre requisite before a grand development programme of the *ummah* is launched is the strengthening of *ukhwah* Islamiah or Muslm brotherhood among Muslims. It is disunity that leads to other problems in the Muslim world such as instability in socio-political and economic organizations, poverty, illiteracy, lack of knowledge particularly in science and technology and the arts. These factors act as obstacles to the Muslims to form a united front to safeguard and maintain the integrity and sovereignty of the *ummah*.

It is important to mention at the outset that the concept of the *ummah* transcends ethnic boundary, political entity, language, social and cultural boundaries. It is not even the same as the concept of society and community in the modern sociological and anthropological sense. Thus the concept of the *ummah* is unique and certainly it can be a very important mechanism in the solidarity of the Muslim *ummah*.

The failure of the Muslim *ummah* to organize themselves as a united front is one major problem faced by them all these years. Without going into the long history of Muslim disunity, it is important for us to realize the need for the Muslim *ummah* to reduce friction and bring about unity among themselves. This has always been the agenda of Islamic movement. With unity, *insyaAllah* our numerical strength can be an advantage. Islamic movement has been a well coordinated movement with the common objectives of producing a socio-economic and socio-political model of development in line with Islamic principles and *shariah*.

There are more than one billion Muslims in the world today but we cannot claim to be a force which can be a threat to others. Islam is spreading very fast in Europe. The Muslim population in the continent has tripled in the last 30 years. Islam is the major religion in the Middle East and some parts of Asia and Africa. There are big Muslim communities in China, the Balkan Peninsulas in Eastern Europe and Russia. Big Muslim immigrant communities are also found in Western Europe and other parts of the world. About 20% of the Muslims are found in Arab countries, 30% in the Indian subcontinents. Indonesia with 15.6% of the Muslims is the largest Muslim country by population. Muslims are majority population in around 30 to 40 countries in the world. The most populated Muslim countries are found in south Asia and south east Asia. Indonesia, India, Pakistan and Bangladesh have more than 180 million Muslims each. In Africa, Egypt and Nigeria have the most populous Muslim communities.

Today there are mosques from Los Angeles and Moscow to Rome and Zagreb. Five centuries after the fall of Spain the azan is heard again in a mosque not far from the old mosque of Cordoba.

Apart from planning various strategies for development Muslims should not forget another important activity that is the *dakwah* movement to the Muslims as well as non-Muslims. By enhancing our effort in the *dakwah* movement, Islam can continue to be understood and spread to the non-Muslims. There have been signs of positive change on the attitudes of western orientalists towards Islam. According to Murad Hoffman in his book Islam 2000 published in 1996 there has been a conscious effort on the part of European academicians to embrace Islam and a number of them are on the brink of pronouncing the *syahadah*. According to the New York Times, 25 % of American Muslims are converts to Islam and around 10,000 and 20,000 people convert to Islam per year in Britain.

We should be optimistic on the rebirth or the emergence of the Islamic renaissance. Islamic organization can play an important role in this respect. As far back as 1926 the World Muslim Congress (*Mo'tamar al-alam al-Islami*) was established in Mecca. Today OIC is providing another mechanism for integration and coordination of the Muslim *ummah*. However we are yet to see constructive results in the effort to unite the Muslims and bring development to them. OIC has drawn up a 10 year development plan for the Muslim *ummah*. The Plan covers development in such areas as intellectual, political, economic, scientific as well as education and culture. OIC is convinced that the Muslims are capable of achieving its renaissance. In the effort to achieve a full-scale development in these areas member states in the organization have committed themselves to achieve (promote) Islamic solidarity in facing the challenges and threats to the Muslim *ummah*. There exists a World Fund for Solidarity and Combating Poverty among OIC member states. This fund if properly administered can go a long way to alleviate poverty in the Muslim world.

OIC can also be a very important mechanism in safeguarding the legitimate rights of the Muslims. Talking about legitimate rights, integrity and sovereignty, how long more do we have to wait until the Palestine issue is resolved. Do we have to wait for another half a century? Without going into the earlier history (1948) suffice it to say that Arab and Palestine territories including

East Jerusalem, the Syrian Golan and the rest of the Lebanese territories are still being occupied. No immediate solutions seen to be in sight. Diplomatic means at all levels have been employed to resolve the issue but to no avail. Even the world body has exhausted its effort to solve the problem. So Muslim countries should be thinking seriously on the need to establish the military industry so as to enable them to protect their integrity and sovereignty.

From the economic perspective, OIC is aware of the abundance of economic resources and potentials in the Muslim countries and these should be exploited to the maximum for development. Intra-OIC trade can be established through a free trade zone and the volume of trade among member countries could be increased to 20% during the 10 year period covered by the plan. Various other proposals have been made such as facilitating movement of businessmen and investors within member countries. The Islamic chamber of Commerce and Industry could also be established to facilitate trade while IDB can play an important role in looking into investment opportunities and intra-OIC trade.

Regarding economic growth for five years 2003-2007 it is noted that only four countries of OIC namely Azerbaijan, Afghanistan, Chad and Turkmenistan show an average growth of more than 10 percent that is between 10.4 to 11.9 percent. For all the 57 countries the average growth is 5.9 percent. 18 of these countries have an average growth between 1.1 to 4.8 percent. They represent 31.5 percent of the total number of OIC countries.

There are three main items which are important in launching economic development in Muslim countries. They are capital, labor and availability of agricultural land. Studies have shown that these are available in Muslim countries. Saudi Arabia and other oil-producing countries can provide the capital. Abundant labor is available in Bangladesh, Egypt, Pakistan and Turkey. Countries like Pakistan, Sudan, Egypt, Turkey, Bangladesh and Indonesia have the potential for economic development but lack of resources. Studies regarding food production have shown that OIC countries could produce 75 million tons of grain in the year 2000 by cultivating only 58 million hectares out of 2200 million hectares available. Land in Sudan alone is capable of being cultivated to produce food for the needs of all the Muslim countries. There are other countries in the Muslim world which can produce coca, coffee, cotton, jute, natural rubber, rice, timber and breeding animals.

Member countries can also be proactive by carrying out Action Plans of their own. This calls for commitment from Muslim countries. One example is an Action Plan to achieve agricultural objectives. In its 25 year Master Plan, the Arab Authority for Agricultural Investment and Development wanted to make Sudan the leading producer in vegetable to be imported to Muslim countries (42%), sugar (20%), wheat (15%), live stock (58%). In 1980 a number of projects were carried out in Sudan in sectors such as dairy, poultry, fruit and vegetable. However no constructive results were obtained and no follow up action was taken.

The Arab Organization for Agricultural development based in Khartoum allocated RM33 billion for the supply of food in the Arab countries. No further development was heard about this although extensive studies have been done in grain, vegetable oils, meat and fertilizer.

The failure in the various projects can be due to various factors. Money or capital alone is not enough. In the case of agricultural projects it is also necessary to involve the farmers. There should also be training facilities and the availability of infrastructures such as roads, power, water supply, marketing facilities, storage and distribution facilities. Above all Muslim countries must be fully committed to carry out the projects so that they do not remain only in the drawing board. This has been the trend do far.

The idea to promote co-operation among Muslim countries so that they can achieve economic independence is really good.

We can be self-sufficient in food and agricultural production. Trade particularly in food and agricultural products among OIC countries can also be promoted. However this needs full commitment from OIC countries especially in implementing the various plans that have been made.

As mentioned earlier in the paper education is another area emphasized by OIC in its 10-year development programme. There is need to increase budget on education in many of the member countries. There is also need to improve education especially in terms of quality.

According to Wikipedia, the free encyclopaedia the public spending in education in the 57 OIC countries is one of the lowest in the world.

Public Expenditure on Education (% of GDP) Some Selected Muslim Countries

Country	1991	2002-2004
Kuwait	4.8	8.2
Maldives	7	8.1
Tunisia	6	8.1
Malaysia	6.1	8
Morocco	5	6.3
Djibouti	3.5	6.1
Guyana	2.2	5.5
Uganda	1.5	5.2
Iran	4.1	4.8
Oman	3.4	4.6
Kyrgyzstan	6	4.4
Senegal	3.9	4

Of the 57 countries listed only the above 12 countries have allocated between 4 to 8.2 percent their GDP as expenditure on education. The rest 45 countries have set aside only between 0.9 percent to 3.9 percent of their GDP as expenditure on education. However in 15 of the countries namely Afghanistan, Brunei, Cote d'Ivoire, Gabon, Guinea-Bissau, Iraq, Libya, Mali, Mozambique, Palestinian Authority, Sierra Leone, Somalia, Suriname, Syria and Yemen data are not available. OIC median in both years are 3.9 and 3.7.

Wikipedia has also listed 10 universities in OIC as scientifically productive universities. They represent only 17.5 percent of OIC countries.

Rank	Country	10 Year Publications	Top Discipline
1	Turkey	82 407	Surgery
2	Egypt	27 723	Applied Mathematic
3	Iran	19 114	Chemistry
4	Saudi Arabia	17 472	General Internal Medicine
5	Malaysia	10 674	Crystallography
6	Morocco	10 113	Physical Chemistry
7	Nigeria	9105	Food Science and Technology
8	Pakistan	7832	Plant Science
9	Jordan	6384	Chemical Engineering
10	Kuwait	5930	General Internal Medicine

In its 10 year Action Plan, OIC has also made a call to encourage research and development programmes in universities. It has been noted that OIC countries have set aside only 2 percent of the Gross Domestic Product (GDP) for this activity. Universities have also been urged to play a more proactive role in the development plans of the Islamic world. Priority should be given to science and technology and there should be a closer co-operation between these universities.

Muslim scientists, technologists and social scientists have a role to play in bringing about development for the Muslim *ummah*. While the scientists and technologists are concerned with bringing new technology, the economists will deal with the purely economic dimensions of development and the social scientists will deal with the non-economic dimensions that focus mainly on the changing of values and attitudes of the Muslims that will be conducive to intellectual, political and economic development. More emphasis should be stressed in the study of Muslim communities and how problems faced by these communities can be solved. Social scientists can be the agents in working for the welfare of the *ummah*. With the religious vision, they will be equipped to solve the problems of the *ummah*.

Early studies of the Muslim communities were done mostly at the dawn of the colonial era by western orientalists as well as local scholars. Most of the studies on the Muslims have been focused on their colonial history and their social, political and economic activities over the centuries. Generally these studies give a negative picture of the Muslims. The western orientalists like to associate them with negative values and attitudes which contribute to their poor conditions such as the Falahan of Egypt or the Muslim farmers of Asia and Africa. They perform poorly in all areas. They are not lacking in rich natural resources such as tin and rubber in Malaysia and oil in the Middle Eastern countries. Although rich Muslim countries have rich natural resources nevertheless they cannot use these natural resources for their political and economic advantages due to their lack of knowledge and skills especially in science and technology. The lack of uniformity in administration is another big problem and in some Muslim countries the administration is so bad that they are more or less in a state of anarchy.

Muslims are not fatalistic as claimed by western orientalists. Of course we have to believe in *Qada' and Qadar*. We have to believe that prosperity is destined by the will of Allah. However we are required to struggle and persevere to achieve success and not to give up at the first sign of failure. In fact, *Qada' and Qadar* is an important mechanism to reduce tension and frustration because of failure in certain ventures. We have to submit to the will of Allah. There is no regret because we have exerted an effort to achieve it.

A lot of research can be done in the areas of health and education and this can also be done by Muslim social scientists. The rate of illiteracy is still high in the Muslim countries and resistance to modern health care is also said to be associated with illiteracy. In this context, social scientists can be agents of change in which they can deal with the human dimension of development.

It is incomplete to talk about development and building the *ummah* without considering the new phenomenon in international relation known as globalization. There are a few questions that need to be asked about globalization. These questions relate to the win-win basis of globalization. Will there be a reciprocal act of giving and taking on a win-win basis. Will Muslim countries have an access to western markets? In what way can the free flow of capital benefit the Muslim countries? Can Muslim countries through globalization share the wealth and technology of the rich countries? Is it not possible for the rich countries through globalization to exploit the resources of the some Muslim countries by using their sophisticated technology and big capital?

With the emergence of the borderless world the west could penetrate into our political and economic systems and would throw Muslim countries into a more serious situation than they suffered during the colonial era. Thus globalization can turn into a process of recolonialization.

After the era of colonialism, Muslim countries have been struggling to maintain political stability and economic independence. Globalization provides a new scenario that may throw states into a further state of disarray and disorganization. In this way, globalization can mean loss of independence and thus the process of colonialization is repeated. We do not seem to have other alternative but prepare ourselves with the necessary skills and knowledge to face the challenges of globalization. This is a big challenge to the Muslim in the new millennium.

This paper has emphasized the following problems that impede development in Muslim countries. They are:

1. lack of knowledge especially in science and technology
2. Political instability and lack of leadership with ummatic vision
3. Economic disorganization
4. Lack of coordination
5. Lack of uniformity in administration
6. Elaborate bureaucratic procedures
7. The idea of the nation states putting stress on ethnic, social, cultural, political and economic boundaries making it difficult for inter-regional mobility and inter-regional co-operation

In conclusion, the following action plans fall into place in carrying out massive development programme for the *ummah*.

1. *Ukhuwwah* Islamiah should continue to be emphasized in the effort to unite Muslim *ummah*. It should supersede other criteria such as loyalty based on nation-states in establishing Islamic identity.
2. OIC countries should be more committed in their effort towards developing member countries so that more constructive results can be achieved.
3. There should be a more concerted effort in carrying out the functions of the various agencies so that there will be

full participation of Muslim countries in decision making and implementation. Development in all its manifestations should be carried out to improve the socio-economic and socio-political conditions of the *ummah*.

4. To cut elaborate bureaucratic procedures to the minimum so that decisions can be implemented without unnecessary delay. There should be flexibility so that it is easier for inter-regional movement of people thus facilitating for smooth mobility of workers within Muslim countries.

5. To tap the resources of Muslim states so that interstate co-operation to attain self-sufficiency in food production and inter-regional trade can be attained.

6. The various existing agencies should be more proactive and consistent in terms of policy making and implementation.

7. Opportunities should be created in member countries to prevent brain drain and migration of highly skilled persons to rich countries. This can also prevent other workers from migrating to other industrialized countries.

No time frame is suggested for the above action plan. It can be a 10 year, 20 year or 50 year development plan. What is important here is implementation. This is the biggest issue. Action Plans of OIC and member countries have been referred to earlier in the paper but to date no constructive results have been achieved. The issue here is not related so much to developmental strategies but rather implementation.

ISLAMIC PERSPECTIVE OF DEVELOPMENT

Jamil Farooqui

This paper deals with different approaches to development. It stresses that development is a broad concept which covers all aspects of human life and society. It rejects the interpretation of the concept in terms of economic and political development only. Thus, the most suitable term to highlight the sense and traits of development is 'social transformation' or 'social development'. Sociologists like Comte, Spencer, Tonnies and Durkheim explained changes in the broad sense covering the whole of society. The paper, further, rejects the contemporary view that changes in material conditions initiate changes in the ideological system including standards of morality, values and virtues. All these should be molded according to the traits of material development. The paper highlights the repercussions of this view. If we allow material conditions to change ideological bases, it will destroy the whole fabric of human relations creating conflict, violence, suppression, exploitation and will damage peace, tranquility and human dignity. The paper sets forth the view that changes and development of material conditions should take place according to the ideological bases and cardinal principles of society. This is supported by the Islamic perspective of development where changes, first, take place in the intellectual set-up and then in material conditions that will increase and be strengthened by the former.

Development is the state of comfortable and dignified living. It refers to the quality of life which, at least, should be adequate or of a high order. It is the condition where members of a society have an adequate opportunity and proper environment to lead a so-called comfortable and dignified life. What constitutes a comfortable and dignified life is a ticklish question because they are subject to space and time and, as such, differ from individual to individual and society to society. Their criteria vary and change according to the preferences and priorities of societies as well as the needs of the time. Thus, development has different meanings to different people. It is a multidimensional term loaded with ideological assumptions.[1] It is generally perceived as a desirable and progressive process[2] associated with raising the standard of living and creating improvement in the general well-being of people, environmental stability and globalization.[3] In fact, its content changes and its meanings alter and it is a continuous intellectual project as well as an ongoing material process.[4]

In the modern age the general well-being of people and comfortable and dignified life, by and large, are considered in terms of material comfort. People should have ample resources and facilities to satisfy their urges and needs in the best possible way or even in a luxurious way. However, these involve abstraction and are difficult to be observed. The same applies to the concept of development. In such cases, social scientists operationalize the concepts and develop certain indicators to make them observable. Rose calls it a 'concept indicator link', considers it necessary and requires care in the movement from the level of abstract ideas to the level of measurement.[5] The development of a society relates to its wealth and, in one way, is assessed through Gross National Product (GNP)[6] and Physical Quality of Life Index (PQLI). The prosperity of a country is measured by GNP per capita (per head) on the basis of mean average. GNP is used when the level of overall productivity of the entire society is considered as the main feature of a developed society.[7] Sometimes the wealth of a country is measured by Gross Domestic Product (GDP) based on all the entirety of the economic activities taking place within a country.[8] Quality of life is again a complex term and involves different criteria. Morris[9] developed an index of 'physical quality of life'. He was conscious of the difficulty due to the different nature of societies but he felt that in developing such an index one should consider that not only one pattern of development is relevant; the values of development are not the same in all societies; it should measure results rather than input; distribution of benefits should not be based on a mean average; it should be simple and it should enable comparison between countries and regions of countries.

Morris, however, constructed the index taking into consideration only three indicators – life expectancy, infant mortality at age one, and adult literacy. According to him, PQLI is based on the mean of a country's scores on these three indicators. All these indicators are problematic, complex and are often contradictory. They are, thus, questionable. The relevance and the problematic issues involved in the index are not here under discussion but they are explained to show that this is the one way of assessing and explaining development which is purely economic. In other words, development is considered synonymous to economic growth. It is but obvious in case we consider that material condition is the only important basis of our lives. In such a case, if a society wants to provide better conditions of living or a better standard of living, it must generate more and more income and spend that on building better infrastructure. Thus, a developed society has to generate more wealth for all and more surplus to provide better conditions of living to its people. It has to boost production, increase trade, business turnover, and all other economic activities necessary to generate wealth.

An adequate economic system or system of generating wealth as well as an adequate strategy to achieve it depends upon an adequate political system that should take care of public welfare, devise an appropriate strategy, create conducive conditions and establish effective institutions to promote economic growth. This will be possible through public representation, accountability of the ruling elite to the public and people's participation in the decision making process. In this context, it is viewed that development in the economic system is related with development in polity. As such, the concept of political development became important and it is thought that economic and political development are interdependent. Coleman observes that "in some cases economic development preceded political development whereas in others political development seems to have come before at least many kinds of socio-economic development".[10] Political development is considered "as the acquisition by a political system of a consciously sought, and a qualitatively new and enhanced political capacity as manifested in the successful institutionalization of (1) a new pattern of integration and penetration regulating and containing the tensions and conflicts produced by increased differentiation, and (2) new patterns of participation and resource distribution adequately responsive to the demands generated by the imperatives of equality".[11]

DEVELOPMENT AS SOCIAL TRANSFORMATION

Development as explained in economic and political terms is not the whole picture of the process. It is, in fact, a broad term and covers all the aspects of society. It should not be limited only to the improvement of economic and political systems but relates to the overall well-being of humans as well as to such a social system that promotes human potential and enables humans to live in peace and harmony, coordinate and cooperate with each other to achieve societal goals. It is a complete transformation of a society where individuals would lead a dignified life in terms of the cardinal goals of society including the spiritual and material. It is a misconception and a distorted view of reality that economic growth or economic development is the remedy for all evils or is the key of all developmental goals. It is, of course, not the 'golden tablet' that can cure all social diseases but creates problems and results in widespread inequality, exploitation and suppression of the poor and weak, affluence at the cost of others and domination of one group over other groups if it does not work and operate under the guidance of an advanced and well- developed moral and ethical system. Economic growth or affluence without the guidance of cardinal principles of humanity destroys the very fabric of human relations and human values. Development means the development of a society as a whole and includes not only economic and political systems but also the nature of social institutions, the structure of social relationship, pattern of culture, nature of values and way of life based on certain cardinal principles and ideals as the goals of human life as well as of society. This we identify as social development which is the transformation of society into a most viable system that promotes and ensures meaningful and dignified living together.

Society is not merely the collection of individuals combined together to meet biological obligations and in this course developed a distinct form but it is a highly systematic collectivity organized for certain cardinal goals and achieving them through a distinct way or method. Society, for this purpose, structures its ingredients and resources, and patterns them in such a way that they could perform functions necessary to achieve the ideals that it cherishes. It, thus, develops institutions and systems that give it a distinct nature and form and for which it is identified and known to the external word. Mukherjee observes that society:

> ...denotes an aggregate of individuals but not a random assortment. The individuals organize

themselves into groups which, at recognized levels of totality, form society... A society is thus denominated the characteristics of the groups the individuals form.[12]

The formation of a human group, according to Mukherjee, is based on two broad principles; the subjective will of individuals and the objective circumstances, and there exists a relation between them that determines the nature of human action and the pattern of society. The relation between the two ingredients of group formation is guided by cardinal values of human life. They are, according to him, survival, security, prosperity and progress. These are interpreted in terms of their operational aspects, that is, how they can be achieved and what ideals one has to observe in the process of their achievement. These are the ordinal values which translate cardinal values into the operational level. He explains:

The cardinal valuation of humankind is differently interpreted in the context of what is appropriate or inappropriate, desirable or detestable, good or bad for humankind. These are ordinal valuations which translate the cardinal valuation with reference to how (and not why) to survive, be secured in life, ensure material prosperity, and attain mental progress. The focus on 'how' substantiates that the four cardinal values are intrinsic to the human species in the light of evolution of life.[13]

The configuration of human society is characterized by the ideals and their manifestations in the thinking and actions of individuals. Society exists and operates smoothly when it maintains a balance between cardinal and ordinal valuations or between subjective will and objective circumstances. It works when society's pattern of maintaining ideals is strong and it adheres to the ideals strongly, dwells on the principles and molds objective circumstances according to the ideals. It is also possible that there would be a distance between the ideals of society and the objective situation. It often happens when the commitments of individuals become weak and they yield to the pressure of the objective situation and mold their action accordingly. If this situation prevails for a considerable period of time, the ideals undergo change and new ideals emerge under the influence of the objective situation. Thus, a new interpretation, a new rationale and new ideas are set forth as a backup to the changes. This situation arises when ideals lose their ground and become ineffective. Durkheim identifies it as anomie. The problem arises when ideals remain the same but individuals are more oriented towards the objective situation due to immediate gain, material benefit and physical pleasure. This creates contradiction and conflict because the ideals and objective situation go in opposite directions and do not serve the required purpose.

Society is a unitary system where all units, organizations, institutions and subsystems work in consonance with the goals set up by society and produce output that is necessary and helpful to operate society as a whole and achieve the purpose of its formation. If changes which are not consonant with the societal goals occur, they damage the pattern of society. Similarly, if change takes place in one unit or in one institution and they fail to act in the desired way and do not produce the desired result, it affects not only the other units and institutions but also mutilates the system as a whole. This does not mean that society does not prefer change and remains static. It wants change that can invigorate the system and make it more and more effective. This generally happens when change commences from within society and is not imposed from outside. In third world societies when the Western model of change in the form of urbanization, industrialization, modernization and globalization were initiated they could not produce the same results which they produced in Western societies.

SOCIOLOGISTS' CONCERN WITH DEVELOPMENT AS A VITAL PROCESS OF CHANGE

Social thinkers from the period of the Renaissance in general and sociologists from the very outset of the discipline in particular have been interested in the study of change in society. They tried to analyze the process of change and highlight its impact on the lives of individuals and on society as a whole. They explained the factors that initiated change and transformed society into a new set up which was, of course, complex, superior and efficient. The historical changes that had taken place in Europe during the sixteenth to the nineteenth centuries have been subjects of analysis and marked as significant instances of development. The motivating factor was the mode of production that was changed from agriculture and handmade to industrial and technological. The establishment of industries and an administrative set-up for adequate governance developed cities as the new social order and new way of life. It had also changed the thinking of individuals, their priorities and preferences. In a nutshell, the rural and traditional order had collapsed and a new one in the form of urban, industrial and modern emerged. Barnett observes:

> The hundred years from 1750 to 1850 was a period of enormous change in Western Europe – change in the ways people lived, and in the way they thought, and, importantly for us, in the ways they thought about how they lived. All the criteria of right and wrong, moral and immoral, even of true and false, were changing as agricultural production changed and large scale manufacture

developed, concentrated into towns and factories, using workers paid with money.[14]

Braudel also highlights the changes that took place in the social structure and way of life in Europe with the development of cities:

> In the changing appearance of cities like London and Paris was reflected the transition from one way of life and art of living to another. The world of *ancien regime,* very largely a rural one, was slowly but surely collapsing and being wiped out.[15]

Similar changes have been observed in other places also and led social scientists to find a theoretical framework according to which changes take place. Comte (1798-1857), following the footsteps of his predecessors, went over the evolutionary process following a different span of time, changing the intellectual framework of individuals which finally culminated in the development of Positive Sciences. He found that positive knowledge changed the mind-set of people who began to think systematically and rationally about their situation as well as about their society and refined them from time to time as positive knowledge developed. As a matter of fact, human society, social patterns and institutions had passed through different phases of development from emotional and authoritarian to rational and scientific or, in his own terminology, from theological through metaphysical to positive. He contemplated that Sociology being a latest development in Positive Sciences can provide 'truth', organize society on positive knowledge and construct a viable, adequate and harmonious social order free from conflict and confusion.

It was, further, viewed that societies in the process of change become more and more complex because they develop specialization and assign specialized tasks to individuals and other parts which make them more dependent upon each other. Herbert Spencer (1820-1903), a proponent of social evolution, spelled out how structures due to the activation of inner or exposure to external forces turn into complex ones. He considered society as an 'organism' and both of them followed the same laws of development. Development in both of them indicates complexity, specialization and dependence. According to him:

> It is …a character of social bodies, as of living bodies, that while they increase in size they increase in structure. Like low animals, the embryo of high ones has few distinguishable parts, but while it is acquiring greater mass, its parts multiply and differentiate. It is thus with society. At first the unlikenesses among its groups of units are inconspicuous in number and degree, but as population augments, divisions and subdivisions become more numerous and more decided …. a social organism and an individual organism are entirely alike.[16]

The important feature of Spencer's explanation is that both biological and social organisms undergo change through the activation, reaction and adjustment of inner forces and ultimately take a new form. Thus, he explained the term 'development' in the sense of development from within.[17] A similar idea had been set forth by Ferdinand Tonnies (1855-1936) when he explained the gradual transition of a society from one stage to another i.e. simple to complex. He observed that moral and ethical bases of society as well as interpersonal relationships gradually undergo change and take a completely new form which is different from the previous one. He characterized two forms of human collectivity as *Gemeinschaft* and *Gesellschaft*. The first one which is, generally, translated into English as 'community' was organized on close ties, shared values and beliefs. It transforms into a more complex one with indirect relationships based on large organizations and governed by law and convention. It is identified as associational society where individual differences pervade it. Further, Emile Durkheim (1858 – 1917) explained the process of change through which society passed in the same way but with the new term 'social solidarity'. Durkheim realized that society has a certain set of ideas, beliefs, preferences and priorities shared by people and which cohere them together. Social cohesion is the force that is manifested in social life and operates society smoothly. He identified it as solidarity and, according to him, it is of two kinds: mechanical and organic. Mechanical solidarity is found in primitive and pre-industrial societies and is based on homogeneity, commonality, agreement and identity of people. Organic solidarity is the characteristic of modern societies. It is "derived from agreement to tolerate a range of differences, conflicts being moderated through a variety of institutional arrangements, such as court, trades unions and political parties".[18] The important point is that Durkheim elaborated how this transformation takes place and which factor is responsible for that. He observed that organic solidarity develops when division of labor exists in society. People used to do different jobs in specialized ways. The specialized tasks which people perform enable them to have differences not just of opinion but also of actions and ways of thinking and living. These enormous differences are tolerated because people require the contribution of many persons in performing the functions necessary to survive and sustain social life. The transformation is based on two important factors. The first is the growth of population that exerts pressure on the means of subsistence as they always grow at a low rate and do not accompany the growth of population. As a matter of fact, competition increases and it adversely affects the moral social order. Society cannot tolerate this ambivalent situation and devises a mechanism in the form of 'division of labor' to control competition and sustain moral social order. The second factor is an increase in the amount of interaction. The greater degree of interaction with greater frequency leads the transformation of mechanical solidarity to organic solidarity and increases greater competition over the use of scarce resources. This can be neutralized with an increased division of labor where some people are responsible for one thing and others for other things. This will minimize the conflict and develop harmony. Thus, society accommodates the social pressure by transforming the nature of its solidarity.

The other significant contribution to the concept of development is made by Max Weber (1864 – 1924). He, in his famous work *The Protestant Ethic and the Spirit of Capitalism*,[19] explained the origin of capitalism which is, according to him, the most rational economic system. He also provided the answer why it was originated in the West and not in other societies. He observed that the major reason is the rise and application of 'formal rationality' in the West. Formal rationality is characterized as "the choice of the most expedient action is based on rules, regulations, and laws that apply to everyone".[20] He cited the example of modern bureaucracy where the rules of the organization decide the most rational course of action. This is the characteristic of the modern West. His major concern was to know what factors develop rationalization in the West and what retard it in other societies. In his cross-cultural studies he found that the factors that develop and retard rationalization lie in religion. He analyzed the role of the Protestant ethic under the influence of Calvinism in the process of development in Europe. Calvinism believed in predestination, and as such, going to heaven or hell is predetermined and people cannot directly affect their fate. They can discern signs of getting salvation from the situation of the present life. One of the major signs of salvation, according to Calvinism, is success in business. This was the reason that Calvinists considered it their ethical duty to achieve success in business. They worked hard and rationally thought about how they could make their business flourish. They did not spend their profit on superfluous things but invested it in the business to earn more profit. As a matter of fact, they emerged as hard, conscientious and good workers because this was the sign of salvation. These Calvinist beliefs are found in the Protestant ethic and that, according to Weber, developed a system of ideas, 'the spirit of capitalism'. This system of ideas induced capitalism. Thus, he concluded that the ethical system led to economic success because it enabled people to seek profit rationally and systematically.

The process of development explained by the above sociologists can be summarized in the following points:

1. Development is a process of change towards complexity, specialization, dependency and efficiency which are, of course, the indicators of a better social order.
2. Development is the modification of the whole set-up of society. It starts from one aspect of society and gradually changes the whole form.
3. Development should start within the system. If it is imposed from outside, it will create contradiction and disturb the entire set-up of society.
4. The way of production is an important factor that initiates changes in society. In other words, creating new means and ways of subsistence affects the pattern of social life and initiates changes.
5. Technology also plays an important role in changing human lives and the structure and function of society.

Keeping these perspectives in view, social scientists have studied different societies, analyzed the process of development and assessed how it takes place. In this context, they categorized societies into traditional and modern or underdeveloped, developing and developed. They advanced different theoretical frameworks to explain how traditional, underdeveloped and non-industrial societies can achieve levels of development. These theoretical frameworks are highly controversial but they manifest the view points of thinkers and, thus, it is interesting to know their apprehensions and appreciation of development and society. The most important among them are given below:

MODERNIZATION THEORY

Modernization theory emerged during the study of the developmental process in cross-cultural situations. Social scientists tried to discover why some societies could not develop and what retarded development in those societies. In the historical context, at the beginning of the Cold War, "the term "Third World" was first used by the independent left in French to describe a "third way" or "third path" between capitalism and communism".[21] During this period, independent states had arisen in the east and did not like to be associated with the partners of the Cold War. They wanted to remain neutral. Their leaders took inspiration from the French, organized the Nonaligned Movement and adopted a separate political path independent of the two superpowers. They pointed out the vast disparity in wealth and power between rich and poor nations and challenged the primacy in the global order of the East-West conflict. They yearned for their own way of achieving the levels of development.

Modernization theory explained the condition of the new states which were (traditional) not conducive to development. They were based on ascribed status, hierarchy, and personalized social relations.[22] In comparison to that, the modern Western world is characterized by social mobility, equal opportunity, the rule of law and individual freedom.[23] These are the traits that facilitate the modification of their structure and enable them to adopt innovation, develop better mechanisms and sets of rules to achieve efficiency. The modern Western world achieved development through the change of the mind- set, development of new ideas, modification of the social order, a new system of work and production. It was thought that the Third World should also adopt these traits, modify its economic and political system and attain the features of modern society. Moore observed:

> What is involved in modernization is a 'total' transformation of a traditional or pre-modern society into the types of technology and associated social organization that characterize the 'advanced', economically prosperous, and relatively politically stable nations of the Western World.[24]

Many other social scientists had similar views and discerned that the Western way of development is most adequate and it should be adopted to remove the backwardness of underdeveloped societies. They appreciated Western ideas and considered them motivating factors to change society, and open the door of progress.[25] Walt Rostow was instrumental in advocating modernization theory. He pointed out five stages of development through which all societies have to pass. These were: (i) the traditional stage; (ii) the preconditions of take-off; (iii) take-off; (iv) the drive to maturity; (v) high mass consumption.[26] He found that the Third World was traditional and, as such, it had to develop the preconditions for take-off which were, according to him, the development of trade, the beginning of rational, scientific ideas, and the emergence of an elite that reinvests rather than squanders its wealth.[27] Modernization theory, in order to facilitate and speed up the process of development, advocated the encouragement of Western investment and the adoption of Western ideas.[28] The exponents of the theory also emphasized industrialization that brought about drastic changes in the thinking of people and the pattern of society in the West. It can also introduce similar changes in Third World countries particularly 'Western ideas of individualism, equality of opportunity and shared values which, in turn, would reduce social unrest and class conflict'.[29] They observe that the commercial-industrial system requires a different set-up, different attitude, different work ethics and different forms of institutions in all aspects of society.[30] Thus, modernization transforms society and achieves the levels of development as Western societies did going along this path.

Modernization theory has been criticized from different aspects. Some challenged the motive of the theory and observed that it was set forth less to remove poverty and more to provide a bulwark against communism. However, the most important limitation of the theory for me, which is more pertinent to the present discussion, is its emphasis on the Western pattern of development either in the form of Western individualism (entrepreneurship) or Western technology (the industrial society). It propounds that both of these forms initiate changes in the social structure and mold it according to their requirements. At the end of the day, social structure emerges in accordance and in consonance with the traits and requirements of Western individualism and Western technology. This is not true empirically. If we study different industrial societies, we find that they have similar technology but they have different social and political structures. One can cite the examples of Japan, France and Britain. All are advanced industrial societies but, as Gallie observes, they have different forms of work organization, trade union structure, cultural relations and, to some extent, political structure.[31] There may be some similarities among them, but we cannot say that technology determines social structure. Besides, there are Third World societies where Western industrial technology was exported but it cannot produce the same results as it did in Western social soil. It has not developed the Western social and political structure that the West developed. Against it the traits of Western individualism and Western technology were adopted within the socio-cultural context of these societies. The result is that, instead of modernization of traditional society the traditionalization or localization of modern values took place. Democracy in the East, instead of establishing peace and achieving progress, created conflict, sectarian feeling, division of people into various groups, tension and chaos.

MARXISM AND DEVELOPMENT

Social scientists, during the study of the process of development, rediscovered another source of thought based on the ideas of Karl Marx (1818-1883), Friedrich Engels (1820-1895) and other Marxist thinkers like Leon Trotsky (1879-1940), Viladimir Lenin (1870-1924) and Mao Tse-Tung (1893-1976). The views of Marx and Engels and actions taken by their followers played a significant role in changing the material condition of people. The Marxian approach was also considered a crucial way to achieve development but it was neglected, on one hand, due to the Cold War and, on the other, due to its critical view of capitalist modernity. Marxian tradition, according to Barnett, was revived in the sociology of development after 1956 when sociologists and social anthropologists worked and studied newly independent societies and exchanged views with their intellectuals. They got acquainted with the Third World intellectuals' views that in the struggle for independence Marxian theory is more relevant, provides a better explanation and guides actions better in comparison to modernization theory.[32]

The theory explains that the process of change and development is guided by the conflict of interest between classes. The conflict is based on contradictions which exist in the basic structure and prevails over all other aspects of society. The major contradiction exists between what a society can produce with all of its potentials and the social relations of production that prevent the potential from being realized. In can be removed when the class that suffers becomes conscious of itself, realizes its position, organizes itself and struggles to change the whole set-up. Thus, social change takes place through struggle and sudden breaks in community. It is not gradual and evolutionary. Kiely finds that it is, to some extent, similar to modernization because it also wants to achieve the goal of an industrial society. The difference is only in the means. He observes:

> ...the Bolsheviks use the state to develop the productive forces. Socialism was defined less by its ability to emancipate labour and more by its ability to develop labour productivity more efficiently than capitalism. It was therefore seen as a different means to achieve the "modern" end of an industrial society based on mass production...[33]

Lenin also emphasized that socialism wants to achieve greater productivity of labour compared to capitalism but in its own way. Lenin said:

> Socialism calls for a conscious mass advance to greater productivity of labour compared with capitalism and on the basis achieved by capitalism. Socialism must achieve this advance in its own way...my Soviet methods.[34]

The Marxist approach similar to Modernization theory, asserts that first material forces should change and develop, and according to that, the human's relation to material forces and other human beings will be molded. Stalin said:

> First the productive forces of society change and develop, and then, depending on these changes

and in conformity with them, men's relation of
production, their economic relations change.[35]

This is problematic because it gives the impression that the
productive forces and generating income are most important and
other aspects and the institution of society are subordinate to
them and work for them. A society which has distinct ideals, a
distinct civilization, a distinct way of life cannot afford to follow
this pattern. It can work only in those societies where the motto
of life is only to satisfy material needs in the best possible way
by hook or by crook.

DEPENDENCY THEORY AND UNDERDEVELOPMENT

Marxist thought became popular and attracted the attention of
sociologists and social scientists from 1967 onwards. They took
inference from Marxian tradition and interpreted the process
of development anew. Andre Gunder Frank severely criticized
the modernization theory and considered it useless because it
failed to understand the social and economic processes at work
in underdeveloped societies. He studied Chile and Brazil in
detail and found that Western social scientists had failed to make
head or tail of the problem of these societies and had incorrectly
identified their problem as one of development. It seems that
development comes about if a society adopts the right economic
policies, work ethics and parliamentary democracy and goes on
smoothly. Frank considers this incorrect and finds it unfeasible.
He pointed out that the process at work in underdeveloped
societies is one of underdevelopment. The relations between rich
and poor nations are not at all beneficial to the poor but they
are destructive, impeding and distorting their development. The
important point is that Frank used the term underdevelopment in a
new way to explain the situation prevailing in poor nations due to
the interaction with their rich counterparts which use and exploit

the poor for their own benefit. Thus, underdevelopment is not the stage that precedes development but it is the result of imperialism and colonialism.

Frank simply explained that the capitalist system polarized the world into metropolis and satellite. The metropoles exploit the satellites through the expropriation of economic surplus which the former use for their own economic development. The result is that the satellites remain underdeveloped because they have no access to their own surplus. He contends:

> My thesis is that these capitalist contradictions and the historical development of the capitalist system have generated underdevelopment in the peripheral satellites whose economic surplus was expropriated, while generating economic development in the metropolitan centres which appropriate that surplus – and further, that this process still continues.[36]

Paul Baran's contribution, in this connection, is also significant. He asserts that the economic relations between developed nations, particularly Western Europe, and the rest of the world are based on conflict and exploitation. The former penetrate into poor nations to exploit their resources and take their wealth. Thus, they take part in "outright plunder or in plunder thinly veiled as trade, seizing and removing tremendous wealth from the place of their penetration".[37] The obvious result is the flow of wealth from poor to rich nations.[38]

WORLD SYSTEM THEORY

The theory was developed as a reaction to and modification of dependency theory. It takes into consideration the different societies and regions of the world in a special historical context

and tries to study their working and the process at work. The
contention that the problem of underdevelopment is the result
of historical relations of exploitation between developed and
underdeveloped societies has different repercussions. It implies
that the development cannot be understood as a problem of
separate societies because they cannot remain unaffected by
the development of the socio-economic systems of the world.
Immanuel Wallerstein highlighted the theme emphatically and
contended that national society should not be taken as a unit of
analysis because it is not a social system. Changes should be
studied in the wider context of the world because the only system
is the world system. He says:

> ...I abandoned the idea altogether of taking either
> the sovereign state or that vaguer   concept,
> the national society, as the unit of analysis. I
> decided that neither one was a social system and
> that one could only speak of social change in
> social systems. The only system in this scheme
> was the world-system.[39]

Wallerstein's ideas are supported by Arghiri Emmanuel and
Samir Amin but in a different way. They tried to explain how the
surplus was transferred to the core from the periphery. Emmanuel
contended that the transfer of surplus took place through a process
of unequal exchange. In this process, the rate of surplus value
expropriated by capital is greater in the periphery than in the core.
This is further affected by the equalization of the rate of profit
in the world economy that leads to a transfer of surplus value
from the Third World to the First World.[40] He accentuated the
wage discrepancies between workers in the core and periphery
that lead to a process of unequal exchange and surplus transfer.[41]
Amin agreed with this view and further assessed "the way in

which periphery's incorporation into the world's economy led to its "extroverted" or "export-oriented" accumulation".[42]

The theoretical explanations presented above have been the subject of severe criticism due to certain critical issues involved in them. One of the major issues is the stagnation of the Third World. It is said that the Third World would be stagnant and cannot develop till they are tied with the core dominated world system. This thesis is not applicable to the Third World which had shown high growth during the 1960's and 1970's. Some considered it a contorted attempt to explain the problem but many agreed that the stagnationist thesis is too strong.[43] Kiely finds three limitations to these theories: "First, they each have a developmental logic; secondly, they each read off changes in the periphery from needs of the core; and thirdly, they share a similar conception of progress".[44]

Developmental logic indicates that people are not important whereas the process of social change is important because it has a predetermined logic that leads society to a particular end. It seems that people are "passive actors" in the operation of historical factors as well as in the alteration and modification of them. Underdevelopment and Marxist theories revolved around capitalism and discussed its role in initiating changes and development. They differ slightly in the result. Gulalp rightly observed that "the terms of the debate are couched within a framework that idealizes the experience of western capitalist development and asks whether or not the idealized experience is reproduced in the rest of the world".[45] The fact is that these theories have not taken into account the forces that shape the history and rise and fall of the communities. Of course, among them the human factor is most important. Humans are not only puppets in the blind social forces but they themselves are the vital force that decides the purpose, direction and path of development.

The other problematic issue in these theories is the relation between the core and periphery. Undeveloped theories consider the core as an obstacle to its development, while the modernization theories consider the core as the promoter of development. Marxism falls either on one side or the other. None of these theories take into account the special historical and civilizational traits and peculiarities of Third World societies that play an important role in establishing relations with the core (in adopting, indulging in and rejecting the traits of the core). These theories, as Kiely pointed out, see "the rest in the image of the "West" which, in turn, can be derived from a common evolutionary position on development".[46]

Thirdly, the concept of progress which these theories adopt is also controversial. Progress for them is economic growth based on the expansion of the market or the development of the productive forces. This is one side of the explanation and ignores the social and ideological factors of a society. It indicates that progress is necessary whatever the cost (social, moral, ethical, physical and ideological) one has to pay. Some societies may follow it but others not. It is evident in the case of the environment where many nations do not follow the path of development because it adversely affects the environment. Moreover, economic growth is to strengthen and facilitate the achievement of the cardinal principles of a society or of an individual life. Thus, it is a means. It cannot be an end and a society cannot afford to achieve economic development at the cost of its fundamental values or cardinal principles.

ISLAMIC PERSPECTIVE OF DEVELOPMENT: AN ALTERNATIVE APPROACH

Development from the Islamic perspective is a holistic concept. It is not limited to economic and political developments only but entails all aspects of human existence. It refers to the overall well-being of humanity leading to perfection and purity of the human soul, body and human's social and physical environments. It is a 'social transformation' in which first, the human mind and soul are transformed to comprehend the "Ultimate Reality", the Creator of the universe, his own self and the material world. Second, the human collectivity is transformed to provide prosperity to humanity in this world and enrich it with high moral standards, virtues and values so as to achieve prosperity in the hereafter.

Islam is a distinct system of life which rotates around certain vital and fundamental principles:

1. The Unity and sovereignty of Allah (*Tawhid*),
2. Humans as servants and vicegerents of Allah,
3. Structure of human relations:

      I.   Human relations with Allah,
      II. Human relations with his fellow beings,
      III. Human relations with other creatures: animate and inanimate.

The Unity of Allah indicates that He is the one, the most sovereign and powerful capable of doing anything which He wants. He created the universe and things living and non-living that exist in it. He established a path, a way on which material or non-living objects work and serve the purpose which He wants. He also created human beings, bestowed upon them superior qualities including the faculty of understanding and provided them guidance through His messengers and showed them clear signs of His majesty and grandeur as well as His management and governance of the universe. He also appraised them of the purpose of human creation, the trust which He thrust upon them, the duties which He assigned to them and the way they have to operate in this world and live in it. If humans follow the Divine guidance, they will get peace and prosperity (*falah*) in this world and in the hereafter. If humans turn away from His guidance, they will face destruction and devastation as well as His wrath.

Humans are created in the best form with superior qualities and as such they are the best among all the creatures. They have been given innumerable bounties and the elements of nature are made subservient to them. They can use them in a proper way to make their lives comfortable in this world. All these privileges have been given to humans because the Creator wanted to take some important functions from them. The function is to manifest the suzerainty of Allah by their thought and action and establish it in every nook and cranny. This is the reason that humans are appointed as the vicegerents of Allah and as such they have to follow His commandments and implement them on earth. Thus, humans are the servants of Allah and they have to completely submit themselves to His will.

Humans, in order to operate in this world according to the Divine order and fulfil the purpose of their creation, come in contact with others: their fellows, other living beings and natural or ecological objects. They use them or get help from them to get their work done, or satisfy their needs or to facilitate their living in this world. Thus, they establish certain kinds of relations with these objects. The relations are, by and large, based on one's psychological and material benefit or the pleasure of one's ego. Consequently, humans do not hesitate to exploit and use those objects for their own benefit even at the cost of the destruction and devastation of those objects. Islam prohibits this inhuman act and impresses upon its followers to behave with them in dignified, judicious and human way. Thus, human relations to others: his fellows, other living beings and material objects, are governed by human relation with his Creator. It means that human should interact with others to seek the pleasure of Allah and not for his own pleasure. As far as his fellows are concerned he should treat them as brothers, help them, support them and should be ready to give them whatever he wants for himself. In case of other living beings humans must treat them with sympathy and compassion, take care of their needs and do not put as much burden as unbearable. Similarly, humans should use natural objects in reasonable and proper way without destroying them and damaging ecological balance.

In the light of this perspective development is human development covering all aspects of human life activating and promoting human potentialities to live in peace and harmony, utilizing Allah's bounties in proper way to facilitate their operation in this world and to accomplish the purpose of their creation.

The other important feature of development in Islam is that development should proceed from non-material aspect, intellectual set up, particularly mind and soul to material aspect economic and political structures and not the other way round. In this respect Islamic perspective of development differs from that of the West. In Western model the improvement of physical world and material conditions are the bases of development. If a society succeeds to improve its material condition or economic system it will develop because other aspects will automatically be changed according to the first. The reason is that changes in material condition will gradually be accommodated in socio cultural and ideological systems and in this process the later (ideological system) will be molded according to the characteristics of the first (economic system). The main concentration in this model is on economic development, generating wealth, increasing production and business turn over and improving standard of living based on material comfort. Islam rejects this model. There are various reasons for this. First, economic development does not give benefit to all sections of a society, to all societies and nations. Only one section of a society, some societies and nations get its fruits and that too at the cost of others. Second, it generates inequalities, divides people into classes, privileged and deprived ones, which often come in conflict with each other. Third, the main purpose of economic activities is to get maximum profit, and as such, the persons who dominate and regulate economic activities and transactions do not take care of public needs and enhance their enterprises at the cost of others. As a matter of fact exploitation and suppression of persons and group take place. The same case is with affluent nations that treat the poor ones as their market, extract wealth from them and retard the development of their economies. Fourth, the rich persons gradually take hold of power, influence political system to adopt policies favorable to them so that they may not only retain their superior position but also expand and enhance their business to other parts of the globe and extract wealth from them by damaging their economies. Fifth, society loses its basic features (ideology and purpose) for which it is known and comes into being if material conditions (economy and its ingredients) are allowed to influence the non-material one. In this process societies, which are only based and oriented to material conditions or which are only interested in the satisfaction of material needs in the best possible way, have no much problem because they do not hesitate to change their socio- cultural and ideological traits according to the changes in material condition. They consider it as an essential condition for development. The problem arises with those societies which have divinely ordained ideological system governed by invariable laws and have definite purpose of their formation because if they will change their ideological bases according to the changes in material condition, they will lose their identity and form. They will face contradiction because there will be a wide gap between their cardinal principles and work. Overall the material condition, or as other scholars viewed, "the immense material wealth has not made people happier than they were before, and it has resulted in a gradual depletion and, in some cases, an outright destruction of scarce ecological and other resources"[47]

'Human development' encompasses all dimensions of human existence. As such, the moral, spiritual and material dimensions are blended into one composite system that leads to the purification and perfection of humans and their socio-physical environment. In this process Islam insists that change in existential condition can be possible when there will be change in their soul or intellectual set up. The Qur'an explains the process of change in the condition of people:

> Verily Allah changes not the conditions of a people until they change what is in their souls.[48]

Similar idea is expressed in different place:

> Because Allah changes not bounty He has bestowed on a people until they change what is in their souls.[49]

These ÉyÉt indicate that changes in the condition of a people are only possible when there is a change in their psyche or thinking. The change in the soul is the harmonization of relation between humans and Allah. It purifies human psyche, develops commitment to truth and justice and avoids indulgence in wrong doing. It enables humans to improve existential condition in such a way as to provide benefit to all people. Thus, in Islamic perspective purification of human intellect leads to changes in material and existential conditions.

Sociologists and social scientists assume that changes in physical environment or in material conditions, scientific innovation, technological production and industrialization bring about change in the thinking of people, overhaul and modify it. If we study these changes we find that industrialization and modern technique of production have been introduced in many societies but they have not produced the same result. Moreover, in many cases these changes have destroyed the social cohesion and led to destruction. Against it, if the changes in existential condition come through the purification of human intellect, they will be beneficial to humanity and provide it strength.

The Qru'an describes two types of changes. One that enhances and increases material condition and strengthens it. It is identified as *tamkin*. The other leads to decline and destruction and is called *ihlak*. Both of these changes are governed by the set and ordained principles. *Tamkin* is possible when people are committed to the values of truth (*haq*) and justice (*'adl*) that is when people purify their intellectual set up and souls. The Qur'an clearly explains citing historical evidences how people and communities have risen up, increased and strengthened their material condition.

> Allah has promised, to those among you who
> believe and work righteous deeds, that He will,
> of a surety, grant them in the land, inheritance (of
> power), as He granted it to those before them.[50]

The Qur'an also explains that people's indulgence in wrong doing (*batil*) and injustice (*zulm*) that is people' failure to change their souls leads to material destruction and decay.

> Generations before you We destroyed when they
> committed injustice; their messengers came to
> them with clear signs, but they would not believe.
> Thus do We require those who sin.[51]

Islam, in the process of development, maintains a balance between intellectual and existential, non-material and material dimensions of human existence. Generally, people neglect the moral and spiritual dimensions when they are too much involved in improving existential conditions. Islam strengthens the spiritual dimension and for that creates an altruistic society that takes care of human lives, improves material conditions and distributes the privileges among individual judiciously and according to fair play.

As far as Allah's bounties or natural resources are concerned Islam stresses its proper and equitable utilization. These resources are the properties of Allah and individuals are only the trustees. As such, they have to be used for the promotion of righteousness and justice as well as for the welfare of humanity. That being so, the Islamic perspective of development as Ahmad views "is directed towards the development of Allah-conscious human being, a balanced personality committed to and capable of acting as a witness of truth to mankind and establishing a society that is just, growing and capable of meeting the real needs of man and society without exploiting others or encroaching upon their rights."[52]

CONCLUSION

The paper examined that development is a multidimensional and value loaded concept and cannot be understood, in proper sense, in terms of economic and political developments. It is better to call it 'social transformation' as classical sociologists highlighted in their discussions of evolutionary and developmental perspectives. It rejected contemporary approach according to which changes in material condition modified ideological system of society. The reason is that it will damage and alter the bases and forms of society for which they are created. Further, material conditions are means and not end. They can be used to achieve the ends. Society has certain cardinal principles according to which all of its aspects, institutions and resources are structured. Development in any aspect of society should be according to those cardinal principles and in such a way as to strengthen them and implement them in all aspects of society. In an Islamic perspective development is overall well being of humanity including spiritual, moral and material dimensions. It commences with changes in souls (perfection and purification of intellectual set up) and proceeds to the increase and improvement of material conditions.

It creates a balance between material and non-material conditions, encourages equitable utilization of natural resources for the benefit of humanity, promotes justice and fair play and helps humans to operate in this world according to Divine guidance.

FROGS UNDER A COCONUT SHELL OR UNDER A GLASS BOWL? PRINT MEDIA, PENINSULAR ORANG ASLI AND DEVELOPMENT

Ahmad A. Nasr

THE ORANG ASLI

The Orang Asli (literally: original people in Melayu language) are the indigenous people of Peninsular Malaysia. They number about 15,000 (1) belonging to eighteen tribes, namely, Semai Temiar Jakun Temuan, Kensiu, Klintak, Lanoh, Jahai, Bateq, Mandriq, Che Wong, Jahut, Semaqberi, Mahmeri, Semelai, Seletar, Orang Kuala and Orand Kanaq. These tribes are classified by the Department of the Orang Alsi Affairs (hereafter: JHEOA) for administrative purposes into three major groups: Negrito, Senoi and Proto- Malay (2). Each has its own language and culture and consider itself different from the others. Similarly, they have varied occupations such as fishing, hunting gathering forest produce, agriculture and/or working for wages and salaries. Most of them are settled and only a small number of the Negrito tribes are semi-nomadic.

During the communist insurgency (1948-1960) the Department of the Orang Asli Affairs (hereafter its Malay acronym :JHEOA) was established to undermine the communist influence among the Orang Asli who, the government realized, provided the communists with food, shelter, information about the movement of the government forces. They also worked as guides and porters to them, and even fought on their behalf. In other words, the communists' survival depended on the Orang Asli. The policy was to regroup the Orang Asli and settle them. The regroupment and resettlement became the basic means to develop the Orang Asli. By this means the Orang Asli could be controlled, and easily reached to receive the basic health, social, educational, economic and other services.

In addition to the establishment of the JHEOA, the emergency also witnessed the Aboriginal Peoples Act 154, which gives some rights to the Orang Asli such as following their own ways of life. It also provides them with Orang Asli Areas and Orang Asli Reserves, and their compensation for what they plant when they are displaced in case the area or the reserve is needed for a development scheme to be carried out by the government, the private sector or even an individual. As such, the Orang Asli reject the government view that it is hard to develop them because of their nomadic life, and they argue that it is the government that makes them nomads by moving them from one place to another.

Like the indigenous people all over the globe, the dispossession of the Orang Asli of their ancestral land is the main problem. The JHEOA, in consultation with the concerned states succeeded in gazetting lands same of them, but sometimes the gazetted lands are degazetted without their knowledge.

The Orang Asli have already one representative in the Senate. By forming associations such as the Peninsular Malaysia Orang Asli Association. Orang Asli started to stand up for their rights (3).

LITERATURE REVIEW

The portrayal of thePeninsular Orang Asli and their development in the print media is almost a virgin field. Mustafa K. Anuar's article entitled "the Malayisan Press and Representation of Minority Groups", and published in 1994 is, to my knowledge, is the only study that deals with the Orang Asli in the Penisular as well as Indiginous people in Sarawak and Sabah as one of three minority groups. The other two are the disabled and the aged. By minority groups he means "groups existing at the margins of socio-economic, political and cultural development". In this preliminary study he points out that the Malaysian government focuses on socio-economic development and emphasizes the people's right to express their opinions on the quality and direction of development- a right which is closely related to the concept of 'Caring Society' prompted by the government at that time. The media, he states, is supposed to play an important role in that respect. He holds that the close relationship between the media owners and controllers and the government together with commercialization and advertising affects the approach and style of reporting. In addition, the print media focuses on important and major events, which are usually related to activities of the major social, economic and ethnic groups and involve prominent personalities and social elite. It is urban biased because the economic and political elites live in urban areas. What is strange and different from the journalistic culture is marginalized from media reporting.

Having said that, Mustafa K. Annuar examines the media reporting on the Orang Asli. He selects two English newspapers, namely the *New Straits Times* (hereafter: N.S.T.) and the *Star* in August 1993 and compares them with those in April 1994. He finds thirty eight news items and articles in the first newspaper and thirty four in the second pertaining to the three minority groups including the Orang Asli in Penisular Malaysia and the indigenous people in Sarawak and Sabah. He finds out that some of the published materials give information about their culture, that the Orang Asli get the press coverage when they become a source of interesting news like being attacked by an animal e.g crocodile, or a disease e.g malaria. They also receive the attention in the press when statements about issues affecting them such as land, logging and tourism are made by a minister, a state chief minister or a politician. He notices that the Orang Asli's opinions in making their village a tourist attraction and its affects on their lives are not reported. Annuar concludes that his preliminary study suggests that due to the relationship between the political elites and media elites i.e owners and hence controllers of media the reporting still holds on to the conventional journalistic practice of giving media prominence only to the social and political elite, while others are always placed at the margins of society and media attention and at times they simply 'disappear'. The news items and articles he examines show that the more complex reality facing minority groups are simply ignored and not covered by the media. He therefore calls for a re-examination of the relationship between the government and media if the minority groups have to receive more media attention (4).

STEROTYPED ORANG ASLI

A Malaysian speaking to the Canadian writer David Lavoie, admitted that Malaysians know so little about the Orang Asli and often have a stereotyped view about them (5). One view, backwardness or primitivism, is sometimes reinforced by writers and reporters in the print media. One writer introduced her article titled "Orang Asli's face always defended" by saying that "when discussing issues related to indeginous people what can imagine is their backward life, poor and imperfect deweling [and] backward [ness] in education". She then points out that the Orang Asli of Swah Batu prefer their traditional life and do not accept development and progress in education – words which confirm their backwardness. Another one writing about animism and animistic practices in the life of primitive people, points out that some Muslims believe in spirits and worship them, as well as several groups of people who have not embraced Islam like the Orang Asli (6). A third introduces his article about the Orang Asli by saying that "[D]istraction, *backwardness* and hard life are normal to them"(Italics added) (7).

Jakun, a name of an Orang Asli tribe, is used by non-Orang Asli when referring to ugly things such as faces and clothes. A presenter in a TV live music award show called his fellow presenter 'Jakun' based on his black classical attire. Other cases were cited, in which the uses of term were insensitive to local culture and beliefs by using it in the incorrect context (ugly things). The reference was criticized by a Jakun senator. The cable television operator Astro officially apologized to the Jakun people especially those in southern Pahang, Johor and Negeri Sembilan on the use of the term (8).

The Jakun are becoming modernized and they will soon lose their culture and tradition. They are no longer the stereotyped indigenous people; they dress like Malaysians, watch television, listen to the radio, drive cars, ride monocycles and speak Bahasa Melayu with English words. Occasionally hunting with blowpipe and darts and collecting forest produce does not mean that they are primitive.

Describing hand fishing practiced by the Orang Asli of Kampong Empang Besar, an Orang Asli activist started his introduction to his article by saying "[T]his is as primitive as it can get", and ended it by "[We] realized we had just witnessed on of the earliest forms of catch fishing". (9). Another reporting about an Orang Asli student who scored 5As in SPM pointed out that her success proved that "less civilization does not mean we cannot be among the extra-civilized people. Sometimes it can be more than that"(10).

Not only reporters,the minister of Culture, Arts and Tourism pointed out that the Orang Asli Museum has the potential to attract tourists and added that foreign tourists might prefer to visit more traditional and *backward* Orang Asli settlements in the country (Italics added) (11).

Because it is "[S]ad to say, we know little about the Orang Asli", the *New Straits Time* devoted one third of a page in the travel section to the description in words and pictures of Orang Asli museum in Gombak, Selangor, to encourage internal and external tourists to visit it and create awareness of the Orang Asli history and culture (12). Three months later, a full report was published in the same section about the museum, whose visit, according to the reporter, is a must for tourists interested in anthropology. The reporter, however, pointed out one shortcoming of the museum, that is giving the number of the Orang Asli as 92,529 (according to 1993 census). Interestingly, he himself gives their number (113,541) according to the 2000 census and not the latest number, and under the pictures of the Heads of the Department we find the caption 'pictures of prominent Orang Asli), (13).

PHYSICAL DEVELOPMENT

a) Electricity and water

The Orang Asli feels that roads, schools, basic amenities like electricity and piped water have tremendously helped them in adapting to the changes of modernization. Ten years ago the Batek Orang Asli were nomads and illiterate, and because they are shy, timid they avoided outsiders. They make it difficult even for JHEOA's officers to approach them.

The officers were not discouraged and could persuade fifty families to settle down and live in houses provided by the Department and assimilate in the rest of society. In 2005 two families have Proton cars, few members have mobile phones and one family has satellite television. "Now they are aware that they cannot escape modernization" (14)

But basic amenities like electricity and piped water were lacking in some Orang Asli communities. For example, most of the thirty eight Orang Asli families in Kampong Juasih, about twenty five kilometers from Labis, still use kerosene lamps, although they live in brick houses. Only one family has electricity after they paid RM500 for the wiring and RM150 for an electricity meter (15).

The Mah Meri villages on Island Palan Carey, which used candles and oil lamps in the past were supplied by piped water and electricity in the year 2002. Only five streetlights were erected in 2005. (16).

The lack of piped water in O.A villages may be due to shortage of water in urban areas. For example, the rapid development of Port Dickson caused shortage of water in rural areas. The Negeri Sembelan state government agreed on a deal, by which Malacca supplies nine million liters. Even before the deal the government installed a pipe water project form Tanjong Agas to Orang Asli Bukit Kuau village. The project costed two million ringgits. (17).

Sometimes the private sector and NGOs join in efforts by various government agencies and JHEOA in providing Orang Asli communities in villages such as Kampong Lubuk, Temenggalan in Negeri Sembelan, with these facilities. As a result the villages do not need to cover a long distance to obtain water and the children would no longer have to study under the dim light of candles. (18).

A reader urged the authorities to get priorities right. Providing 247 settlements with electricity and 335 with piped water after more than half a century of independence should come before sending a Malaysian to space. Orang Asli, according to him, "have been neglected. They need urgent help to advance socially and integrate with the mainstream society to prevent further marginalization, isolation and alienation in a fast changing world".

(19) Another, who has been involved with the Orang Asli for a number of years and who defended their cause by word and deed, points out that the Orang Asli Mahmer community of Carey Island were provided with electricity and water supply during the election and after a RM 17000 donation from Tun Dr. Siti Hasmah Mohd Ali in 2003. (20).

b) HEALTH

Another approach of the JHEOA to develop the Orange Asli is to improve their health and wipe out infectious diseases. It, with the assistance of several agencies, implemented what it called the medical evacuation system, whereby very sick or injured living Orang Asli in remote settlement and those facing death could be airlifted to a centre where they get medical treatment and survive. One center, the biggest facility of its kind, covers four states, namely Kelantan, Pahang and Perak and serves more than 50,000 Orang Asli. Among the served ones are pregnant women who prefer to deliver at government hospitals. In 2002 the centre served 1,609 patients; in 2003 1,313 patients and in 2004, 1394 patients. (21)

The infant mortality rate which was high when Orang Asli gave birth at home, has greatly dropped due to the facilities provided by the Ministry of Health and the Department. Children are also healthier because of the treatment provided by clinics and visiting teams. But to give birth at the center-cum-health clinic or a hospital a Temiar women from Simpadel village has to endure a painful process, which entails a four-hour walk through the jungle from her village in the remotest interior of Kelantan to Pos Belah. Here she has to wait until her husband finds a means of transport to take them to the Orang Asli transit centre at Kuala Petis after covering a six-hour journey partly in dirty roads. From Kuala Petis a mother may choose to go to clinic Desa which is run by the Ministry of Health or the Orang Asli clinic, which is run by the Department. If the case is urgent the mother will be sent by an ambulance to Gua Musang, which is thirty kilometers away or to the Orang Asli Hospital in Gombak, Selangor. All these difficulties are "a walk in the park compared with what [The Orang Asli Women] had to endure in the past" (22). The clinic also checks health of women during pregnancy and advise them what to do to improve it and how to take care of the babies and the importance of bringing them regularly for check up and immunization. (23)

Kosmo tells of the experiences of an Orang Asli who came for treatment in Pos Buntu Rural Clinic at Rauls, Pahang and the nurse working there. It tells how the Orang Asli were first sceptical of modern medicine but had to discard their scepticism and shyness specially when coming face to face with the outside community, in order to receive medical treatment. The nurse, who has been there for four months, was initially nervous when posted in that remote clinic in the interior and thought that problems of communication and culture would make her work harder. But she found that the Orang Asli would give their utmost full cooperation especially after befriending them. In fact, she is beginning to enjoy her work (24).

Both the Rural Development and the Health ministries are working toward upgrading the health of the Orang Aslis. The health programme includes proper infrastructures like housing, clean water supply and toilet hygiene.

JHEOA has various partnership programmes with corporate bodies such as May Bank, which donated a sum of RM 1400 for medical equipments to the Orang Asli Hospital, whose several of its staff including nurses and a doctor are from the community itself.

An Orang Asli one-day health medical and dental camp was organized by the Serhya Sai Baba Central Council of Malaysia, Pahang branch of the Malaysia Medical Association, the State Health Department and the Rotary Club of Kuantan. Thirty seven doctors, forty nurses and sixity volunteers participated in the camp at SK Kedaik's hostel complex at Kedaik. The camp served the Orang asli of Kedaik and the surrounding settlements, about sixty kilometers from Kuala Rompin. More that eight hundred Orang Asli benefited from the camp's medical treatment, and screening for hypertension, obesity, diabetes, hearing and eye problem, and an examination of teeth and bone densities. The doctors referred several people to the nearby hospitals for further examination and treatment (25)

The Colgate – Palmolive Company and the Malaysia Dental Association collaborated in organizing a health of mouth programme. Orang Asli of Kampong Sungai Yol, Raub, Pahang were unaware of the side effects of using charcoal to clean their teeth, a practice they inherited by generations. They were instructed on how to take care of their teeth and the necessity to make regular check-ups. The company seized the opportunity to donate toothbrushes and toothpaste to them (26). In addition, the Royal Army organized a four-day health programme called "True Heart Project" at Kampong Jeran Kedah, Ulu Beranang and Lenggeng in Negeri Sembilan. The programme provided medical treatment including circumcision of ten children aged between ten and twelve years old (27).

TOURISM

One of the approaches adopted by JHEOA to improve the Orang Asli's life was to make them aware of their culture and art for the purpose of tourism. By that it hoped to develop a good market for their handicrafts and to achieve this objective by joining efforts with various tourism and handicraft promotion organizations. (28). Tourism is a topic highlighted by the print media as another source which can be tapped to increase the income of some Orang Asli communities. It reports an individual's NGO's and state government's attempt in this respect.

NST tells the story of an Indian Malaysian who lived with the Jakun for almost two decades and helped them to improve their living standard. His plan was to put the Jakun youths in touch with their cultural heritage as a way of promoting social development. He applied for one of Ford Conservation and Environmental Grants and received a total of RM 22,000 to carry on his project in Malaysia. He used the money to build a cluster of traditional house to serve as accommodation for tourists.(29)

The private sector such as DiGi Communication company organized a programme to protect the heritage of an Orang Asli community Mah Meri in Carey Island. The programme targeted a number of children who were divided into two groups. The first group(20 children) is taught how to make traditional musical instruments from mangrove wood and play them while the second (40 childern) were taught woodcraft. The programme was conducted by an activist and expert Orang.Asli, who is involved in the protection of Mah Meri culture for the last twenty years (30).

The Semai village Ulu Geroh has been the site of the Malaysian Nature Societies Raffles in Conservation and Ecotourism project since the year 2002, because their natural environment is a haven home for rare and beautiful bird wing butterflies known as Raja Brookes. The society is assisting the villagers by publishing their social interdict skills with local and foreign tourists and this cash in on tourism. In the past villagers sold butterflies to middle men who framed the species to sell each at a price ranging from RM 30 to 500. As more tourists are visiting the village, the society opened an information centre in the village (31).

In the year 2002 the Malacca state government decided to diversify the tourists' attraction by developing Orang Asli settlements as tourism products. It intrusted a company to implement the project by selecting Orang Asli settlements at Gopan, Jasin where 114 families live.

Kampong Orang Asli Suku Temuan in Bukit Kepong, Pasir Panjang, Negeri Sembilan has been chosen for attracting tourists because of its strategic location and beautiful surroundings. A culture and handicraft centre, a long house and a performance hall were built. This would allow the tourists to experience the life style of Orang Asli and become familiar with their traditional food (32).

More than one thousand Suku Batek communities also attract tourists because they live at the edge of the National Park in Penang while others live far inside the forest and practice their traditional life (33).

Orang Asli Sungai Kajar village in the middle of Belum Draja forest Grik, Perak is also attracting local and foreign tourists by its lake, which has many species of fish, beautiful scenery and beautiful handcrafts and traditional way of life (34).

Traditionally, the Mah Mer community in Coorey Island used the woodcarving they make as rituals to protect their lives in the sea. Toady they sell them to tourists and use them as ornaments. The Temior Orang Asli of Kelantan make traditional headgears of rattan, tree bark and wild flowers, believe that they protect them from spiritual and bodily harm, and indicate a man's status in his community Now they sell them to tourists (35).

The skill of making traditional handcrafts is transmitted from father to son.

While the prestige and profile of handicraft are increasing, raw materials are getting scare and the number of skilled elder producers is declining continuously. Their skill has to be transmitted to the interested young. The need to learn what the market wants and quality control are important. Government agencies like the Malaysian Handicrafts Development Corporation, under the ambit of the Ministry of Entrepreneur Development have to promote the manufacture and more importantly the marketing of handicraft. Villages need to form co-operatives. NGO's can also play a role by buying the products and remarketing them overseas.

"SPIRITUAL" DEVELOPMENT

Orang Asli associate professor Juli Edo estimates that 30% of Orang Asli are Muslims, 15% are Christians, and the rest have indigenous religions (36).

Compared with other issues, religion is rarely dealt with in the print media. But the Muslim Orang Asli's celebrations of Ramadhan (the month of fasting), and 'Id Alfitr are reported. For example, the Muslim Orang Asli of Temetong villages, who embraced Islam in 1985, celebrate the month every year in spite of their poverty. In 2006 eighty new converts joined in fasting. The villagers stressed the benefits of fasting and the needs they expected from the Governement and Islamic Organizations (37). A visit to or an outreach programme targeting the Orang Asli villages is also reported. An example of the first is the visit of Wilayah Persekutian Perkim *du'at* to Orang Asli villages to preach Islam, celebrate Ramadhan and 'Id Alfitr and at the same time welcome the new converts and strengthen relationship with them (38). An example of second is the one-day outreach programme organized by Islamic organizations in collaboration with Majlis Agama Islam in the State, in which twenty one volunteers from Persatuan Kebagsaan Pelajar Islam Malaysia (PKPIM) and Majlis of Selangor participated and targeted the Orang Asli of Hulu Tamu, Hulu Yam. The objectives of the programme were to celebrate the coming of Ramadhan and to train Muslim students to identify the means to present da'wah to non-Muslims especially the Orang Asli. That day seven Orang Asli embraced Islam (39). Another outreach programme was organized by the Department of Islamic Development and collaboration with the Federal Territory Islamic Council and held at Kuala Sayap settlement at Hudu Besut, Terengganu for one day. The aim of the programme was to expose Orang Asli women to modern life including make-up and have decoration (40). Another was organized by the All Woman's Action Society and Peninsular Malaysia Orang Asli Association on the International Women's Day at Kampung Sg. Judah in Carey

Island The Community was educated on issues like rape, domestic violence, child sexual abuse,and women were informed about their rights (41).

The celebration of all Orang Asli of Perak of their new year regardless of their tribes or religions is also reported. The festival, which the city folks admire because it shows Orang Asli's cultures and traditional music, dance and crafts, was originally called Genggulang and involved praying to the spirits to protect villages from bad luck and evil. But in the year 2002 the *batins* (chiefs) decided to exclude the animistic practice and call it Jispai to accommodate the Muslim and Christian converts. (42)

However, the issue of religion was extensively covered when the state of Klantan declared its campaign to convert the Orang Asli to Islam. The state government was not satisfied with the number of Orang Asli who embraced Islam. Out of 12,000 Orang Asli in the state only 2909 became Muslims. To reach its target the state government established in the year 2006 a separate *da'wah* unit to focus on converting more Orang Asli to Islam. Six missionaries joined the new unit. To motivate *du'at* to join the unit, it announced that a missionary would be given material incentives in the form of ten thousands (10,000) ringgits to enable him to marry an Orang Asli woman and settle down permanently in an Orang Asli community to spread Islam, act as a spiritual model, as Imam, teacher of Qur'an and Fardu 'Ain and perform funeral rites. Thus, by having a family relationship, a missionary would be fully committed. Other incentives include free housing, a one-thousand ringgit monthly allowance, and four-wheel-drive vehicle. By giving such incentives to encourage the missionaries to reside in the said communities the Kelantan government would overcome some of the problems of the *du'at* such as the short visits paid in the past and lack of follow-up of conversion and solving the problems which a new convert may face. In other words, the incentives would guarantee the continuity of missionary activity. Moreover, the missionary may be able to acquaint himself with the local culture and learn the local language and use it in communicating the Islamic principles. In addition, his children will be raised up as Muslim (43).

The announcement of the incentives was immediately followed by a number of objections. The human rights commissioner considered the conversion incentives as an "abuse of power" and that inducement or reward for conversion, especially of vulnerable and marginalized women in the Malaysian society, was unethical and unacceptable from any religious perspective (44).

The Director-General of JHEOA criticized the Klenatan government's incentives to *du'at* to marry Orang Asli women on the ground that such marriages lack sincerity – a basic characteristic in Islam, and that it is better to use the financial incentives for Orang Asli education and for improving their welfare (45).

Almost a week later, NST gave a two-page coverage of the topic in the spotlight in the prime news pages under the title "Are they, The Orang Asli, Losing their Cultural Heritage?" with a quotation from the interview with Orang Asli Professor Juli Edo. "They [the Orang Asli] do have a religion. They believe that there is a God and that they are spirits". In addition to Professor Juli Edo, the reporter also interviewed Dr. Colin Nicholas (46).

Juli Edo noticed the declining number of young Batek and Mah-Men in participating in the annual festival to play homage to Halak- the spirit of honey and fruit and ancestors of the Carey Island tribes. He added that change of faith also affects handcrafts and that art of weaving, in which spiritual motifs are used, is also dying because the motifs are against their new faith. Adapting the motifs to suit the new faith, according to him, "boarders on sacrilege". Even Orang Asli languages, he opined, are in danger. Some missionaries, are encouraging Orang Asli children to switch from their mother tongues to Bahasa Malaysia in order to facilitate their work. Language, he said, is an integral part of identity and plays an important role in social cohesion. Conversion also disrupts the harmony of society for the new converts look down on their 'pagan' and superstitious brothers and elders.(47)

A representative of POASM opined that "[i]t is not the role of the state to convert people. The state should recognize the Orang Asli traditional belief as religion and stop all attempts to convert them". The POASM is planning to set up an organization for the Orang Asli belief similar to the Hindu Sangam but he admitted that the setting up of such an organization to manage Orang Asli spiritual affairs is not an easy task because the eighteen tribes have different practices and rites and are geographically separated (48).

EDUCATIONAL DEVLOPMENT

In January 1996 the Ministry of Education took over the jurisdiction of the ninety five Orang Asli primary schools from JHEOA. In 2003 it amended the Education Act 1996, whereby parents who fail to send their children to primary school are liable to a maximum jail of six months or RM5,000 fine or both. (49). The Ministry also adopted a new approach to narrow the educational gap between the Orang Asli and other communities by modifying the syllabus at schools of large number of Orang Asli students and giving specialized training for teachers. An Orang Asli Education Excellence was established at SMK Lepas as a model for other schools. A hostel was built to house students from remote settlements.(50) It is noteworthy that when the Ministry of education took over the responsibility of the primary education of the Orang Asli it directed the Curriculum Development Centre to review the Orang Asli curriculum in a way that help Orang Asli pupils master reading, writing and arithmetic skills. The Centre designed the module of several core subjects to make them meaningful and relevant to the Orang Asli environment. It found out that using folklore to teach basic skills was very effective. (51).

The Department continues to provide the Orang Asli with school fees, school uniform including shoes, ration and stationary as well as scholarships for higher education. In the year 2005 for example, a total of RM 11,200,640.00 was allotted for these educational facilities. But some Orang Asli parents, such as those of Tanjung Sepat village, complained that the school uniform and shoes were not given in time, that they were received in the middle of the year and shoes sometimes did not fit. The eight ringgits JHEOA paid directly to school for every child were sufficient in the past. Schools have raised the fees which the Orang Asli cannot afford to pay. (52) In an interview, a twenty five year old Orang Asli said that he dropped out of school because his family was unable to support him financially and he had to turn to a part-time job like carving wood in a workshop. The fees include health insurance, donations for extra curriculum activities such as remedial education, computer decoration, pupil incentive fund, and workbooks. (53).

The Department continued to cater for the dropouts who are not interested in academic education. It, in collaboration with the industry provided training courses for Orang Asli youth to gain a skill and therefore earn a better income. Such training programme includes construction, automotive technology, tailoring and computer literacy. In 2004, for example, 295 Orang Asli youth benefited from these training, and a workshop was organized to assess the programme and formulate projects for 2005. The Ministry of Rural Development, on the other hand, placed those who are not interested in academic qualification in community colleges that provide skill training. (54)

In Pahang, the Department of education is aware of the difficulties for Orang Asli to register to the special education for those who are living in the rural settlement or the behaviour of the parents who do not register their children in that programme. Other factors that lead to drop out are: far distance to school, low socio-economic background, negative perception of parents and children, and influences of culture. Holistic approach to handle the problem (55)

The Ministry of education is so keen to make education accessible to the remote Orang Asli areas that material for constructing these schools for Orang Asli communities in Lanjon, Titum and Lemai in Pahang were transported by a helicopter for lack of roads to the three villages. As a result the cost of constructing each school rose from RM2.4 million to 24 million. The question NS.T. asked was why the roads were not built before the Ministry implemented the project? Also the Ministry provided the schools with computers and science laboratories at a time there was no electricity (56).

The dropping out of school continued. Transport is one of the reasons cited by some Orang Asli communities for the dropout. Students have to travel long distances to their schools, and sometimes it is too much a hassle to walk to the main road to take the school bus. In other cases, they have to cover about an hour –journey by boat as in the case of school children of Jahai, a sub-group of Negrito living in Sungai village, Kejar Hilir. Once, thirteen villagers including students drowned. (57). Other reasons are being unable to adapt to the outside world such as the students from Kampung Juasih, which is about twenty five kilometres from Labis, or being traumatized by the taunting of their classmates who look down on them and consider them primitive and uncivilized (58).

The dropout rate is also attributed to the unwillingness of the students' parents to relocate by joining the accessible settlements. They are so much emotionally and spiritually attached to their remote traditional settlements that they find it hard to abandon them. Thus Orang Asli communities in Kampunh Tahan, were urged by the Deputy Prime Minister on his visit to move to the nearest settlements for the good of their children (59). The parents' attitude towards education is also mentioned as a reason for the huge rate of dropout.

The order of the reasons in terms of significance may vary from one Orang Asli community to another. For example, a researcher from U.K.M conducted a research among Orang Asli students dropout from primary school, who constitute almost half of the student i.e 646 of those who could not make it to the secondary school. The main reasons, he found out, are boredom and indolence. Other reasons include lack of interest (5.61%), being scolded by teachers (10.1%) helping parents (5.61%), inferiority complex (4.41%), far distance from school (3.8%), peer influence (3.8%) and financial problems (1.9%) (60). it is noteworthy that the researcher listed what he thought to be the reasons for the dropout and did not include non-encouragement by parents, and being traumatized by the taunting of class-mates, and lack of interest.

The Ministry introduced several measures including building hostels, constructing roads and improving the existing ones in settlements in an attempt to reduce the number of dropouts and improve class attendance (61). In addition, the Ministry of Rural and Regional Development allocated million of ringgits for sponsoring transporting O.A students from the interior and for their meals (62).

Print media also highlights the success of Orang Asli students who excel in STP and SPM examination every year as a means of motivating other students and indirectly telling them to take those successful one as models, emulate them, and follow their advice. For example *New Straits Times* carried the photogragh of a thirteen year old Orang Asli girl and her parents, and reported how she scored 5As in her UPSR and consequently received a bicycle, RM200, a school bag and a certificate of appreciation from the Deputy Prime Minister in an appreciation ceremony organized by the Malaysian Examination Council. In an interview with her, she advised Orang Asli students to get rid of the inferiority complex and strive for excellence (63).

The highlighting of Orang Asli success is not confined only to primary and secondary school students' achievement but also includes Ph.D. holders and business men to show that long hard struggle pays off. Information is given about the first Orang Asli PH.D. holder,Juli Edo who got his degree in Anthroploghy from the Australian National University in 1999 and working at present as an Associate Professor at University of Malaya. The second is the computer scientist Dr. Bahari Belaton, who received his degree at the University of Leeds and joined University Science Malaysia. The third O.A. Berjaya received his degree from UKM in 2006, became the head of a section in Fisheries Department relevant to his speciality in the Ministry of Agriculture and Agro-based industry. A long interview is carried out with the fourth one, Dr. Bah Pian, who speaks of his long hard but fruitful education journey. He tells of his poverty striken background, his walking four miles to primary school with no pocket money and coming back home hungry to eat Tapioca, his being the only one to continue at a time all the children in his village dropped out of school when they were in standard three. The determination and hard work, encouragement from family, teachers and lecturers and financial assistance from JHEOA paid off (64)

The success of an Orang Asli businessman such as the founder and chairman of Pahang Kijang Mas Company, of Orang Asli Bikit Rok Bera, is also highlighted. In an interview he attributed his success to his parents' concern for his education and the support of JHEOA. He hopes that the Minister of Education could appoint and train more teachers from his people and send them to Orang Asli villages. By doing that the ministry will motivate children and people around because these teachers know the Orang Asli cultures, languages and problems better than the outsiders (65).

Access to newspapers is limited due to illiteracy and living in the remote villages. Radio is more practical and far cheaper than television; it has become an important medium of communication in rural areas according to Colin Nicholas,coordinator of the Centre for the Orang Asli Concern. Asyik FM, which started its half-an-hour operation from Radio Malaya Federation Building in

Kuala Lumpur on 2nd February 1959 to stop communist influence on Orang Asli, is now broadcasting its program from 9am to 10pm using the languages of the two biggest Orang Asli tribes i.e.,Semai and Temiar. In addition to Temuang and Jakim, every month Asyik FM would visit an Orang Asli settlement and record their music, songs and traditions and by this way they managed to collect one thousands classic songs. What concern us here is that every program or segment includes an aspect on self development, education and health. (66). Though concentrating on entertainment, Asyik FM is preserving Orang Asli heritage.

The increasing awareness of the Orang Asli parents of the importance of their children's education is reported (67). Such parents are even ready to send their children to school not using the Malay language as a medium of instruction. About 140 children in the Cameron Highland are attending a Tamil school because it is the only one near the settlement. They could pick up the Tamil language, communicate in it and understand most of the lesson. Language is not a problem. The only problem according to the head master of the school is transport for they have to walk about three kilometres. He contacted the JHEOA officials of Cameron Highland to solve the problem. (68) Bah Pian blamed the Orang Asli on their attitude towards education. "If the Orang Asli wanted to move forward they must change their mindset"(69). Also the Orang Asli representatitive, Osman Bunsu opined that their negative attitude toward education would push them deeper into poverty, and cited as an example the primary school dropout, and the very small number of Orang Asli professional- four doctors and one professor (70).

The high dropout is not due to the Orang Asli culture, and students' and their parents' attitude according to Colin Nicholas. He holds that poverty is the major obstacle. He notices that the school begins in January, and Orang Asli are expected to bear the fees and other expenses in November and December which are the wettest months of the year and the most financially difficult months for the Orang Asli parents. In addition rubber yield is usually low during these months and collection of forest produce is dangerous and not in demand. He opined that since the Orang Asli are lagging in all aspects behind the other communities, Orang Asli students cannot compete with others who enjoy better facilities, additional tuition and have best teachers and parents who can afford the education expenses. Bright Orang Asli students, he adds, could not join the Tertiary institutions because of the meritocracy policy. He holds that the affirmative policy which worked out for the Malay such as former Institute Technology Mara (now University Technology Mara) and Mara Junior College could also be applied to the Orang Asli.(71). NST reports the Deputy Prime Minister words about the possibility of setting us a Mara Junior Science College for Orang Asli most likely in Pahang, which has the largest number of Orang Alsi. Such college he hoped would reduce thedropout and improve their educational prospects. The qualifications for enrolling in the College will be tailored to suit the Orang Asli students (72)

The effort of individuals, NGO's, and the Ministry of Education to motivate the Orang Asli parents are also highlighted by the print media. An example of individual concern with the high rate of dropout and need to motivate the Orang Asli children and their parents is an Orang Aslichairman of parents-teachers association of SK Pos Handrop. He has a secondary school certificate and could easily get a job but he preferred to stay with his people in Tuel village,Gua Mosang in Kelantan and make sure the younger generation do not dropout and be left behind. He uses to address pupils, whose age is between seven and twelve, every month when they come back from the school hostel to the village, while their parents watch and listen. He advises them to study hard, increase their productivity, listen to their teachers to achieve what they wish to be – a doctor or an engineer, for example. He also tells them to socialise with peoples from outside. He usually ends the assembly by reciting the following words:

Dengar Selalu Nasihat Ibu (always listen to mother's advice).
Patuhile Nasihat ayay (follow your father's advice).
Agar beroleh berkat hidupmu (so that your life will be blessed)
Di Dunia dan di Akhirat (in this world and the Hereafter). (73).

A five-day outreach programme (18-23 september 2006) on 'Special Education and Visit to Settle the Education Problem of Orang Asli' targeted the biggest Orang Asli settlement Hini, Pakan, Pahang. The programme was organized by Japatan Pendidikan Khas Kementerian Pelajaran in collaboration with other government agencies, higher educational institute, NGOs and launched by Professor Madya Jul Edo. The Orang Asli parents were informed about the importance of their children's education. The programme also gathered information about Ornag Asli education, culture and traditions (74).

The Rotary Club of Bander Utama, Petaling Jaya, Selengaor organized a fund raising dinner in Kuala Lumpur on 14.1.2008 to help the hunter gatherer Jehai Orang Asli community in Perak, especially their children. The club members' original intention in visiting the Belum national Park at lake temonggor in Ulu, Perak was to experience the beauty of nature. In the process, they interacted with the Jehais and realized their sad plight. The members agreed with the Jehai elders to provide education for children below fifteen years with basic education including books, stationary and food while attending classes. The club also engaged education experts to make a simple syllabus for this long-term project, which is expected to continue for three to five years (75).

HARDCORE POVERTY

Poverty is still a problem for the Orang Asli. At the end of the year 2003, 22, 967 Orang Asli were classified as "hard-core poor" (76). Poverty was emphasized by the representatives of the Orang Asli Community in the Senate, Osman Bungsu. He pointed out that 50% of them live below the poverty line and the percentage is expected to increase due to the surge in the cost of living. (77). No wonder then that aid in the form of food and clothes and sometimes cash is distributed to them by individuals, NGOs, private sector and/or government.

The Government Society Department of Ampang Jaya City Council gave this kind of aid to seventeen Orang Asli families in of Kemensal Village. The aid was contributed by the private sector and Ampang Jaya residents. In addition stationary was given to school children, and each family received RM 200 (78)

Visitors to semi-nomodic Jahai-a subgroup of Negrito helped them with rice and sugar. But giving aid is a temporary relief of poverty. Food would be eaten, clothes worn out and cash spent and the Orang Asli would remain among the hard-core poor. One of the vision of the JHEOA is to eradicate hardcore poverty among the Oang Asli by the year 2010. The economy and infrasocial development division within JHAEOA plans to eradicate poverty by 2020. The question is how? Land ownership could help eradicate such poverty, accordance to Nicholas Colin. Orang Asli can work on their own land for a better standard of living. The lack of land has deprived the Orang Asli of assets or capital ownership. On 7th August, 2005, the political secretary of the Minister of Rural and Regional Development informed the general meeting of the Orang Asli Association that a national policy on land ownership by the Orang Asli was in the pipeline in consultation with JHEOA (79)

LAND

Land is the major problem of indigenous people all over the globe. The Orang Asli in Peninsular Malaysia are no exception. The problem was highlighted by NST twice- in 2006 and 2008 by focusing on the legal battle between the state of Selangor and Orang Asli Sagong Tasi and six others over a 1,532 hectares in Kampung Bukit Tampoi, Dengkil, which the state acquired to build the Kuala Lumpur- Nilai highway in 1995. The newspaper reported that it was officially declared that the Orang Asli in the Peninsular do not have exclusive land rights, that the state government's ownership of that land is derived from the Selangor Sultanate in 1766. In addition, Temuan could not give evidence that their ancestors had been occupying the land before it became the Sultanate's property.

On September 14, 2005, the Court of Appeal upheld the decision of Shah Alam High Court that the Orang Asli Sagong Tasi and the six others are the customary owners of the land. But the Federal Court rejected the argument that considers the Aboriginal People Act 1954 is a fundamentally human right statute and therefore acquired a quasi- constitutional status. This, the Federal Court argues, is a broad and liberal interpretation of the Act. Hence, the Orang Asli concerned have no right over the land itself but on the items on it and there were to be compensated for those items under the Land Acquisition Act 1960, and on the Aboriginal Peoples Act 1954. The case of Adong bin Kuwan and others versus Kerjaan Negri Johor and others, which went to the Federal Court was cited. In that case, it was decided that the compensation to the Orang Asli was only possible for what was in the land. It is noteworthy that after March 2008 election a new state government of Selangor was formed from Parti Keadilan Rakyat, DAP and PAS. It instructed its legal advisor to ask for a postponement of the case as the government needed more time to study the issues. The newspaper hinted that the Orang Asli may get-out-of-court deal. (80)

The decision of the Appeal Court, the newspaper noted, would apply not only to land gazetted as Orang Asli reserve but to those occupied by them, and would have serious financial implications on the States and Federal Government. (81)

Deforestration adds to the woes of the Orang Asli because it affects their environment, deprives them of economic sources and self –sufficiency and threatens their livelihood. Some two hundred Orang Asli living in Kampung Juasih, about twenty five kilometres from Labis complained of the pollution of their rivers and deforestation which are eroding their way of life. In the past they had no problem involving a living by collecting the jungle produce and no fear of going hungry because rivers of the jungle provided them with what they need. Now they are reduced to working as labourer. They collect for middle men and the work is seasonal; they have no land of their own. No wonder then that they sometimes protest and lose or win. Their protest is reported by the print media. In one case more than 350 Orang Asli of Kampung Bukit Rok and Kampung Iban demonstrated for six hours as a protest against logging their ancestral land, and erected a barrier at the entrance of the centre to stop logging. They opted for such an action because the two police report they lodged and the complaint they sent to the office of Menteri Besar of Kuantan and their repeated request for help from their wakil rakyat were to no avail. They claimed that JHEOA recorded their ancestral land as covering 2023.37 hectares. Menteri Besar questioned this figure and added that the true extent of their reserve was much smaller but did not state the actual figure. "Of course, we can't give each Orang Asli family 50-60 ha", he said. He also pointed out that the logging company had licence and that the logging was part of cleaning land for an agricultural project. The forested area was estimated to produce about 1,000 tons of timber. The Menteri Besar claimed that this Orang Asli community have been living off the concerned area for generations and that this led JHEOA to record their ancestral land as covering 2, 023.47 hectares. (82). In another case the protest of the Orang Asli had positive results. For example, in June, 2003 Temuan Villagers of Kampung Sg. Miak in Bentong, Pahang protested the logging near the village to make way for the development of a fifty hectares piece of land. The logging, they said, would affect their source of water and traditional orchards. They set up a blockage to prevent the logging contractor from continuing to construct a logging road into the concession area, and consequently they were arrested. In reaction to the protest the Pahang government cancelled the project. (83)

Sometimes the Orang Asli seek a legal solution in court. Construction of dams in Orang Asli areas, where they had lived for centuries is considered in their view, one of the obstacles in their development especially that the energy is not directly supplied for them. In the year 2007 twenty four Temuan and three Senoi sought a court order to postpone the Kelan Dam project in Raub, Pahang. The respondent was the Director-General of the Environment Department Pahang State government and the Federal government. (84)

Another group of Orang Asli from Kampung Sungai Buan, Rampin filed an application for judical review at the High Court seeking the abolishment of the state decision to approve part of their land to TH Plantations for development, and the declaration of their customary right to their land (85)

Even the reserve Orang Asli land is sometimes used by outsiders for commercial farming without Orang Asli's permission. One affected Orang Asli is that of Kampung Dusun Pekan, who complained to the Pekan District Office and the Pekan branch of JHEOA but to no avail. In the end fifty of them had to stage a protest and thus attract the print media's attention, and the representative of the Orang Asli in the Senate who said he would contact the Office and the Department before taking any action. (86)

Those who claim that the Orang Asli cannot claim the ownership of their customary, argue that (i) the National Land Code does not recognize this kind of ownership and (ii) that the land outside the gazzeted land reserved to the Orang Asli is "state land and therefore the state has the right to release it to developers". Referring to a disputed land between Orang Asli Teuman and their state, a reader refuted such an argument because the common law practiced in the local courts does recognize Orang Asli's right to their customary land, and he cited two cases in support of his view. Such cases, he added, are considered as part of Malaysian law according to the Federal Constitution. He urged JHEOA to explore "the possibility of the existence of common law Orang Asli rights over the disputed land and help them pursue legal action".(87)

ORANG ASLI and POLITICS

About 70,000 Orang Asli nationwide were eligible to vote in 2008 elections.(88) The print media encouraged the Orang Alsi to participate in the election. For example, a seventy-year-old Orang Asli woman, who never failed to vote, urged the Orang Asli to emulate her. She followed up the latest issues before voting on T.V. bought by her son, a successful contractor whose studies were financed by JHEOA. "It will be [a] waste not to vote. After all, everything is available including transportation to the pollying station," she said.(89) In election time some politicians make pledges to the Orang Asli and forget about fulfilling them once they are elected. An Orang Asli from the Mahmeri tribe, of whom 500 of them have the night to vote, advised their elected representatives not to talk too much, but to go ahead and help them if they want to. (90)

It is noteworthy that only Muslim Orang Asli are full member of UMNO, they can vote in UMNO general assembly and hold offices. The non-Muslims are associate members and do not enjoy this privilege. UMNO encourages the Orang Asli to form branches. Thus the Orang Asli full members have another channel for their problems and aspirations [in addition to JHEOA because UMNO provided an effective platform for their concerns (91).

But not all politicians make promises to the Orang Asli during the election time and do not show up after that NST highlighted the efforts of an elected representative of a rural constituency in Perak state. His constituents include about 5,500 Orang Asli. He emphasized his efforts to persuade the Orang Asli who were still leading a nomadic life to stay in permanent modern settlements to have access to amenities such as clincs, pipe water, electricity, schools, roads and community halls, and to urge elders to enroll their children in schools.(92)

The print media also reported the impact of the political crises in the state of Perak in early 2009 on the Orang Asli's issues. In 2008 election the opposition won Perak state and formed the government, which took significant resolutions affecting the Orang Asli, and in which the Malaysian Bar and NGO, were involved. The resolutions included the cancellation of all logging and plantation activities which affected 2000 Orang Asli settlements in Gopeng, the return of 16 hectres and 200 hectres ancestral land, which were earmarked for logging activities and for a botanical garden by the previous government respectively. A task force committee consisting of two tiers was formed to recognize formally all customary land of Orang Asli in the state of Perak. It is noteworthy that the Orang Asli communities manage the second tier and were provided with venues in The State Secretriat Building where they could hold their meetings. (93)

A few months later the government formed by the opposition lost its majority due to the resignation of three of its supporters and was replaced by an UMNO government. The Malaysian Bar, which put the above issues on record, hoped that the new government would continue with the same previous government's spirit and called upon all states to give more concern to the issues of the Orang Asli and the marginalized. (94)

The new government of the State, however, opted as the print media reported for the soft strategy, that in providing Orang Asli community in Batang Padang with more houses for the hard core poor, and with clinics, schools, piped water, electricity roads and a community hall. The government allocated RM13 million for the amenities in addition to RM 6 million to JHEOA to develop them under the Ninth Malaysian Plan. (95)

ORANG ASLI and the INTERNATIONAL DAY OF INDIGENIOUS PEOPLE :

In December 14, 1992, Malaysia, as a member of the United Nations joined the other states in the United Nation Declaration for the Rights of Indigenous People (DRIP). The Representative of Malaysia in the United Nations insured the world in his address in the opening ceremony that "the interests and rights of the people [The Orang Asli] as citizens and as a group with special needs are protected by the constitution and The Aboriginal Peoples Act, 1954". In 2001 the Prime Minister stressed the same point. "The Government has been sensitive to the rights and needs of The Orang Asli for a long time".(96) But The Orang Asli think otherwise. On The Indigenous People International Day (97) dressed in their traditional dress, about one hundred and fifty members of Jaringan Orang Asal SeMalaysia, a ten-year old Indigenous People.

Network of Malaysia (JOAS), planned to march to Istana Negara to submit a memorandum to the King, urging the government to honour the United Nations Declaration for the Rights of Indigenous People. The nine-page memorandum included, among other things, the demand to establish an Orang Asli native court, abolish the laws which marginalize them and to stop leasing their customary land without consulting them, violation of rights to self-governance, and pressure to assimilate. The group was forced to disperse by the police on the ground that their representatives had failed to obtain a permit. JOAS president and two other representatives briefed the media on the contents of the memorandum, and that its handing over to the King was a symbolic gesture. They rejected their labeling as anti-development and anti-establishment, and emphasized their rights to their ancestral land and pointed out its sacredness and relationship to their identity. In other words, JOAS wants the government to implement DRIP. (98). A week earlier the President of the Bar Council made the same demand, i.e that "the Government must look into the interests of the minorities because Malaysia had adopted the United Nations Declaration on the Rights of Indigenous People" (99)

On 21.9.2008, the deputy Director- general of JHEOA responded by focusing on its effort to solve the problem of land in collaboration with the Peninsular states' governments because land is a state affair, and pointed out that 20,000 hectars had been gazetted for the Orang Asli, and another 31,000 had been approved while applications for 80,000 were still to be considered. He dismissed the demand for a special court because the Orang Asli as citizens are subject to the same judicial system.

The Director- general of JHEOA described the foiled march as an attempt by certain NGOs which are linked to international groups "to hijack the Orang Asli agenda to portray themselves as heroes championing native rights…, (that) the Orang Asli who had been influenced by them had nothing to do with it. The Orang Asli are easily influenced".(100) In a letter to the editor of NST the president of the Indigenous People Network of Malaysia responded to some of the Department's comments.

Quoting Alah Beling's words in 2007: "I am not instigated by anyone; I am instigated by my own stomach", he rejected the Department; accusation that they were influenced by some NGO's. The Orang Asli, he said, "had a lot to do with that march". He found "it insulting that in this day and age the department still thinks of the Orang Asli as being unable to make up their own mind and that, if we are not convinced by the department's policy, we must have been influenced by some other body". He invited the Department to engage with their organization for a dialogue about the issue and to study the DRIP. He pointed out that Orang Asli's issues need to be discussed openly, and ended by thanking NST for its coverage of these issues (101)

The Director -general of JHEOA reacted to letters to the Editor of NST from Colin Nicholas and Adrian Lasimbang. He reaffirmed the human and physical development carried by the Department, the generous compensation paid by the Government for the Orang Asli, whose land had been taken over for developmental projects, and how the agricultural projects initiated by the Department depended on the villagers' consensus. He also pointed out that the Department had always sought the co-operation of NGOs, and hoped that the public would not be confused by inaccurate statement about the Orang Asli's issues made by other parties. He concluded his response by saying that "[t]he JHEOA will ensure that the interest, well-being, prosperity and advancement of the Orang Asli in Peninsular Malaysia are protected" (102)

It is noteworthy that when the JHEOA responded to the foiled march two full pages in the N.S.T focus section were devoted to the efforts of the JHEOA to develop the Orang Asli. The first page mainly highlighted the Department's effort in the field of education which is "much more than physical development, is the way forward for this minority group".(103) Also important figures were given in physical development (housing, roads, electricity, water, health, entrepreneurship, organized settlement, and land development). Most of second page was devoted to the biography of the Orang Asli Nisra Nisran Asra Ramlan, who made history by becoming in 2008 the first deputy Director general of the Development. "[H]e is now the man in charge of making sure development projects, worth hundreds of million ringgit, benefits the lives of the natives the same way his has been aided". (104) Ramlan was intrusted with the budget for physical and human development of the Orang Asli. He dismissed some of the stereotyped view about them an the need to deal with their social problems such as HIV/AIDS, prostitution and drug addiction.

The two pages, under the main title "JHEOA: Pillar of Orang Also Community" were undoubtedly meant to boost the image of the Department in the eyes of the readers and to counter the words of the representatives of the foiled march of the Indigenous Peoples Network of Malaysia to submit their memorandum to the King.

It is also noteworthy that as a result of the incident two reports and a letter to the Editor of NST concerning land were published. The first report is about giving land titles to 10,000 Orang Asli in Perak. This news was announced to the reporters by Datuk Ngeh Koo Ham after chairing a meeting attended by the government departments and Orang Asli organizations.(105) The second report concerns the nern of land to a 1000 Orang Asli community of Kampung Chang Sungai Gepai. The attended land was earmarked by the Federal Government for a fifty million ringgit national arboretum without consulting the community, but later it decided not to proceed with the project for financial difficulties. The state government decided not to entertain other parties' interest in setting up the arboretum. The community got back its land with the help of the Bar Council. (106).

Referring to JOAS unsuccessful attempt to hand over their memorandum to the King, Terence Gomez, associate professor of political economy at University Malaya, answered in an article the question raised by the incident, namely why indigenous people of the world are losing out in spite of the international charters and national laws that assert and protect their rights. The answer, he opines, is in the conflict in the interpretation of the term "development" by the indigenous people on one hand, and that by the governments, multinational corporations, and international financial institutions such as the World Bank and the International Monetary Fund on the other hand. For the indigenous people land is the main issue, it is the right to their ancestral land and "their view survival as a community". The governments aim at the eradication of poverty and providing a better life for the citizens, the international financial institute gives the funds for the governments to fulfill their goal and "support for long-scale exploitation of natural resources including oil and mineral deposits, privatization programmes and the construction of huge infrastructure projects especially dams". Due to that, he argues, the legislation of protecting indigenous people's rights unless they are included in the political system and participate in making decisions affecting their lives. This is explicitly stated by a member of JOAS: that the Orang Asli are not against development and that they want to be included in the decision making. (107)

CONCLUDING REMARKS

What Anwar has said in his preliminary study on the presentation of the Orang Asli, (including the natives of Sarawak and Sabah) as one of the three minority groups is to some extent valid. The Orang Asli make news when the Prime Minister, his deputy, ministers, high officials and/or politicians speak about issues affecting them. The Orang Asli receive attention in the print media when they themselves become a source of interesting news like being fined RM300 for hunting a protected species (palm civets) because this was one of the rarest cases (108) or the Orang Asli girls who disappeared were suspects of being kidnapped but later found to be working as house maids.(109) Anwar's claim that the Orang Asli's views on tourism and its effects on them are not reported is true but, as we have seen their views are reported, especially when they stand up for their rights to their ancestral land, or march to hand over a memorandum including their demands to the Sultan in the United Nations International Day of Indigenous People.

The print media as Annuar points out is urban biased. Some of the news items are initiated by the reporters themselves out of interest (what make good news). In other cases it seems they are invited by an NGO or government department which has outreach programmes to the Orang Asli, or by JHEOA.

The news items are sometimes accompanied by expressive pictures that demonstrate the poor condition of the Orang Asli, usually adults sitting in front of a traditional house with his/ their child (ren). The items come under attractive titles to draw the reader's attention and make him read them. Example of such titles are "Help, yes but don't talk too much", "Helping hand for forgotten people".

The news items are usually published in the inner pages.(110) Only when the issue is sensitive, like religion, that it is dealt with in the spot-light page. It is noteworthy that Colin Nicholas' claim that the budget allocated to the development of the Orang Asli does not go to them is reported in the bottom corner of a page where it is hardly noticed by the readers. It comes as no surprise then that the JHEOA did not respond to this serious claim that amounts to accusation of corruption.

Only few readers write letters to the editor of NST about the Orang Asli and the problems of their development. Those who write are ones concerned with this minority group such as the president of the Malaysian Bar, M. Ganeshadeva who described himself as one being involved with the Orang Asli and defended their cause by word or deed, and Colin Nicholas the Director of the Centre for the Orang Asli Concern. No editorial in NST. is devoted in the years examined to the Orang Asli.

It is noteworthy first that the Peninsular Orang Asli, unlike the natives of Sabah and Sarawak and the Malay art culturally defined in terms of language, customs, traditions and way of life, and are *not* considered as bumiputra. As such, they do not enjoy the benefits allocated to the Malay and the natives of Sabah and Sarawak. Secondly, the Islamisation of the Orang Asli figures out very clearly in the mission of the JHEOA in 1993: "The Department will always be working to implant *Islamic values* to the Orang Asli groups as a way to integrate these people into the general community".(111) However, later the policy was changed. The JHEOA's mission is "to ensure that the Orang Asli community achieves a level of socio-economic well-being at pair with those of other communities in this country, and imbued with *ethical values* while at the same time maintaining their identity". (Italics added).

In 1997, the Director-general of JHEOA expressed his disappointment on the false accusations and criticism made by foreign journalists and academicians regarding the Orang Asli and the influence of these foreign reports on local media. He identified twelve areas that fall under these accusations, namely the claim that the Orang Asli are the first Indeginous people of Malaysia, Islamization and assimilation, the weakness of benefit of Bumiputra, Orang Asli Act, the lack of Orang Asli in managerial posts within JHEOA, land tenure, lack of consultation, education, poverty and exploitation of Orang Asli. He claimed that the reports covering these areas were inaccurate and did not reveal the real condition since these foreigners stay for a few months and pretend to be experts in the field. He argued that Malays and natives of Sarawak and Sabah were also indigenous people, and claimed that there was no official policy of Islamization and assimilation of the Orang Asli. He also pointed out that there was no qualified Orang Asli to fill in posts in JHEOA and likened the demand to appoint Orang Asli in the Department to the demand to appoint fishermen in the fisheries department. He added that the JHEOA would be ready to take local journalists to the jungle if it was approached.

The twelve issues enumerated by the then Director-general of JHEOA are still covered by Malaysian reporters. Whether or not their reports are inaccurate and influenced by foreign journalists and academicians can be determined by comparing the material published at that time and today. Suffice it to say here as examples that since that time there is some improvement in the Orang Asli conditions, that some of them are given land titles in spite of the fact that they are not considered bumiputra and that today the Deputy Director-general of JHEOA is an Orang Asli.

The Deputy Minister of Rural and Regional Development expressed his disappointment that the Orang Asli community in Sawah Batu had not responded to the millions of ringgit spent by the government on building homes and setteling up oil palm plantation to assist them in earning a living and have a stable income.(112) In spite of what the government has done for them to improve their lives many still do not realize or understand these efforts, and can not accept development and progress in education, and feel comfortable with their traditional life. He urged them to work hard on their palm oil and rubber plantation and not to rent the land to foreign workers.(113)

A reader rightly pointed out that the government should not impose what it wants on the Orang Asli, that it should identify what they themselves want to improve their lives and thus make development in line with their cultures.(114) In other words, the Orang Asli are like "frogs under a glass bowl rather than frogs under a coconut shell," to quote an Orang Alsi *batin* (chief) ; they want development that aims at eradicating poverty. This depends to a large extent on a review of development policies, mainly by abolishing development imposed on them (rubber plantation, for example), giving them land titles and identifying how they themselves want to be developed.

NOTES
* Thanks to my students who translated the Malay newspaper cuttings into English.

1. The Orang Asli representative in the senate estimates their number in the year 2008 as 141,230 (N.S.T., 14.12.2008) whereas, the JHEOA gives the number as 149,723 according to its senses in 2004. (JHEOA Annual Report 2005, p.67)

2. The Proto-Malay label, which is used by JHEOA, should be discredited according to Lye Tuck-Po because it suggest that "the Orang Asli are incompletely evolved Malays." The term is derived from R.O. Winstedt's dual classification of Malay groups, namely proto-Malay i.e the first wave of

Malays and Deutro-Malay i.e second wave Malays (Tuck- Po Lye Orang Asli Peninsular Malaysia: A comprehensive and annotated bibliography CSEAS Research Report Series No 88. Kyoto, Japan: Centre for Southeast Asian Studies, Kuyoto University, 2001) p.218

3.   For more information see Collin Nicholas' The Orang Asli of Peninsular Malaysia, Petaling Jaya, Selangor: Centre for the Orang Asli Concern, undated.

4.   Mustafa K. Anuar, The Malaysian media and presentation of minority groups, *Sojourng,* 9 (2), pp.200-212.
     For list of newspaper references see Saleh Hood (ed.), Orang Asli sebagai bahan berita 1974-1986 (Orang Asli as news, 1974-1986), unpublished check list of newspaper references, Bangi: Universiti Kebangsaan Malaysia, 1986, and Colin Nicholas, Anthony William-Hunt and, Tiah Sabak," Orang Asli in the news: The emergency years 1950-1958", Petaling Jaya, Selangor: Centre for the Orang Asli Concern, 1989.

5.   David Lavoie, "Orang Asli and the first nations", N.S.T, 9.3.2008.

6.   *Berita Harian,* 20.8.2006

7.   Idris bin Musa, Visiting Non Muslim Area, *Harian Metro,* 24.11.2006

8.   N.S.T., 17.4.2003

9.   Casey Ng, Look ma, bare hands!, N.S.T, 4.11.2008

10. N.S.T., 28.3 2006

11. N.S.T., 27.12.2002

12. N.S.T., 9.7.2008

13. John Tiong, All about the Orang Asli, N.S.T, 4.11.2008

14. Rasli Zakaria, Batek tribe now at ease with modernity, N.S.T., 17.2.2005
15. Neville Spykerman, Woes of the Orang Asli, N.S.T., 9.10.2005
16. N.S.T, 9.10.2008
17. *Utusan Malaysia*, 11.9.2006
18. N.S.T., 31.5.2003
19. M. Ganesadeva, get priorities right, N.S.T., 26.2.2008
20. Datuk Anthony Ratus, It's Orang Asli who need the break, N.S.T, 26.2.2008
21. N.S.T., 11.2.2005
22. N.S.T., 13.2.2008
23. N.S.T., 12.2.2008
24. *Kosmo*, 17.1.2007
25. N.S.T., 8.7.2006
26. *Kosmo*, 12.7.2006
27. *Berita Harian*, 18.3.2006
28. N.S.T., 3.1.1993
29. N.S.T., 10.10.2005
30. Wan Jailani Razak, Budaya Mah Meri Diputihara (protection of Mah Meri Culture) *Berita Harian*, 23.6.2006
31. Shahrul Hafeez, Orang Asli cash in ecotourism, N.S.T., 11.8.2006
32. *Utusan Malaysia*, 11.9.2006
33. Riadz Radzi, Suku Batek lebih unik (Suku Batek is more unique), *Harian Metro*, 7.12.2006
34. D.J. Dolasoh, Hidu Tenong di Kampung Sungai Kejar (living in peace in Sungai Kejar village), *Harian Metro*, 4.1.2007
35. Sam Cheong, Heads, they win, N.S.T., 27.4.2006
36. N.S.T., 11.5.2006

37. Haris Fadilah Ahmad, Masyarakat Orang Asli Pidrap bantuan (The Orang Asli Community Needs Help), *Utusan Malaysia*, 25.9.2006

38. *Harian Metro*, 24.11.2006

39. Khairul Anuar Musa, Mahasiswa menyambut Ramadan bersama Orang Asli (The Graduates celebrated Ramadhan with the Aborigines), D*ewan Siswa Magazine*, 22.9.2006

40. *Berita Harian*, 16.8.2006

41. N.S.T,

42. Carey Ng, Orang Asli party, N.S.T, 5.2.2008

43. N.S.T., 27.6.2006

44. N.S.T., 29.6.2006

45. Chow Kum Hor, Cultural heritage? More Orang Asli are leaving their ancestral beliefs behind, N.S.T., 5.7.2006

46. Ibid

47. Ibid

48. Ibid

49. N.S.T., 9.1.2005

50. Shahrum Sayuthi, Orang Asli education gets much needed boost, N.S.T., 24.9.2006

51. N.S.T., 28.3.1998

52. N.S.T., 9.1.2005

53. Ibid

54. *The Sun*, 10.9.2001

55. *Kosmo*, 15.9.2006

56. N.S.T., 15.3.2003

57. N.S.T., 30.5.2008

58. Shahrum Sayuthi, Op Cit., N.S.T., 24.9.2006

59. N.S.T., 22.1.2006

60. N.S.T., 19.11.2005

61. N.S.T., 24.4.2006

62. Deborah Loh, Orang Asli rally behind top scorers, N.S.T., 28.3.2006
63. N.S.T., 28.3.2008
64. N.S.T., 6.8.2006
65. Ramli Bin Dollah, Orang Asli Berjaya,
66. Kosmo, 18.1.2007
67. N.S.T., 13.8.2008
68. Chandra Sagaran, Camerons Orang Asli children attend Tamil schools, N.S.T., 11.2.2005
69. N.S.T., 13.8.2006
70. N.S.T., 14.12.2008
71. N.S.T., 13.8.2006
72. N.S.T., 9.1.2009
73. Adham Shadan, (The spirit of Alang Pendak), Kosmo, 6.6.2006
74. N.S.T., 24.9.2006
75. Francis Dass, Helping hand for a forgotten people, N.S.T, 23.1.2008
76. Badrul Hizar Ab. Jabar, Orang Asli dapatbantu (Orang Asli received aid) *Berita Harian*, 22.12.2008
77. N.S.T., 14.12.2008
78. N.S.T., 22.12.2006
79. N.S.T., 8.8.2005
80. V. Anbelagan, Orang Asli may get out-of-court deal, N.S.T, 15.4.2008
81. Ibid
82. N.S.T., 18.4.2006
83. N.S.T., 2.6.2003
84. N.S.T., 12.2.2007
85. N.S.T., 29.11.2008
86. N.S.T., 14.12.2008
87. S. Yogeswaran, They do have rights over land, N.S.T, 18.2.2009
88. N.S.T., 20.2.2008

89. M. Hamza Jamaludin, Orang Asli, what a waste of you to not vote, N.S.T, 16.2.2008

90. N.S.T., 20.2.2008

91. N.S.T., 11.5.2006

92. N.S.T., 3.1.2009

93. Ambriga, Sreenevasan, A leg-up for Orang Asli, N.S.T, 12.2.2009

94. Ibid

95. Ivan, Loh RM 13 million for Orang Asli: Development funds to benefit Batang Padang Community, N.S.T, 9.3.2009

96. N.S.T., 12.11.2001

97. Evangeline Majawat, Police stop march for Orang Asli rights N.S.T, 14.9.2008

98. Ibid

99. N.S.T., 6.11.2008

100. Chai Mei Ling, 20,000ha gazetted for Orang Asli reserve, N.S.T, 21.9.2008

101. Adrian Lasimbang Orang Alsi had a lot to do with the march, N.S.T 25.9.2008

102. Mohd Sani Mistam, Orang Asli get full aid from the dept, N.S.T, 10.10.2008

103. N.S.T., 21.9.2008

104. Ibid

105. 105.N.S.T., 9.10.2008

106. Jaspal Singh, Orang Asli win bid to keep land, N.S.T, 6.10.2008

107. Terence Gomez, Why indigenous people of the world are losing out, N.S.T, 5.10.2008

108. M. Hamza Jamaludin,Orang Asli proacher fined,N.S.T.,1.1.2009.

109. 109.Marc Lourdes,Missing Orang Asli girls found missing, N.S.T.,9.2.2008

110. The Orang Asli news was covered once on the front page which is usually reserved for major attention news. That was when the then Prime Minister said that the "Government wants to upgrade the standard of living of the Orang Asli without changing their culture and tradition" N.S.T., 23.6.1999

111. N.S.T., 3.1.1993

112. N.S.T., 3.5.05

113. Nurashigin Umar,O.A's fate is always defended' *Berita Harian* online 30.8.06

114. N.S.T., 9.5.2006

THE IMPORTANCE OF SELF-REALIZATION IN HUMAN AND SOCIETAL DEVELOPMENT ACCORDING TO MUHAMMAD IQBAL (1877-1938)

Adibah binti Abdul Rahim

INTRODUCTION

Muĺammad Iqbāl was born on Friday, November 9, 1877[1] at Sialkot, and died on April 21, 1938 at Lahore. He was one of the Muslim thinkers, who emerged in the early twentieth century with his idea of reconstructing the religious thought in Islam. In his process of thinking, Iqbāl pondered over all the fundamental system of the Islamic way of life including *Sufism* so far as the doctrine of *waĺdat al-wujËd* was concerned. However, he could not reconcile this doctrine and the true spirit of Islam. Therefore, he revolted against it, and introduced a unique philosophy of *khudi* or selfhood. Iqbāl's philosophy of *khudi* or self is the most significant view to be discussed because it is the central idea

---

[1] There has been a confusion regarding the exact date of Iqbāl's birth. Some writings stated 1873 and 1876, but the most popular correct data was 1877.

of his philosophy on which the rest of his thought-structure is based. This philosophy of self has been found in Iqbāl's works in Persian, *AsrÉr-i-khudi* and *Rumuz-i-Bekhudi*². *AsrÉr-i- khudi* was translated into English version by Professor R. A. Nicholson from Cambridge University under the title *Secrets of the Self*. It deals with the philosophy of the self, or the individual personality, and contains the central theme of Iqbāl's philosophy. *Rumuz-i -Bekhudi* was translated into English by Professor A. J. Arberry under the title *The Mysteries of selflessness*. It deals with the individual in relation to his society in an Islamic state. Then, the idea of self has been subsequently developed in all Iqbāl's poetical works, and more systematically in his lectures, *The Reconstruction of Religious Thought in Islam*.

SELF-_NEGATION IN OTHER RELIGIONS

Iqbāl's deep and wide knowledge of sociology and the history of different culture convinced him that the main responsibility for Oriental decadence was due to those philosophical systems which inculcated self-negation, abnegation, and self-abandonment. These systems instead of encouraging man to overcome the difficulties of life weakened his moral fiber by teaching him to seek peace in running away from the difficulties. Most of the important religious systems of the world can be divided into two groups, Hindu and Semitic. All Hindu religious systems preferred ascetic inaction to a life of struggle. Meanwhile, Semitic religions like Christianity and Judaism also came to adopt a similar outlook since early in their history. Their religious systems essentially appeared practical in outlook, and dynamic in thought, but by passing of time, this system became corrupted. Under the impact of Hellenic thought, it began subscribing to the theory of self-negation and self-effacement. This theory encouraged man to run away from the difficulties of life instead of grappling with

---

² Both were published in 1915 and 1918.

them, and engendered a feeling of other-worldliness which led people spending all times in thinking of the joys of Nirvana. Life is regarded as a mere illusion, and nothing in life seemed worth striving for. These thoughts led to ill-conceived system of pseudo-mysticism. Iqbāl, in this sense, was clearly opposed to Buddhism and Hinduism teachings, which taught a way of escape from life, because Nirvana, according to them, is total cessation of existence. In Buddhism, life is essentially evil and individual existence is miserable in its depth and root. Thus, it teaches withdrawal from all kinds of existence because it is essentially evil, and that human personality is the very center of human miseries. Hence, the self-feeling and personal existences have to be denied[3]. Iqbāl's opposition to these views is clear throughout his discussion on the concept of self.

IQBĀL'S CONCEPT OF SELFHOOD OR KHUDI

Iqbāl has done detail studies about the history of the world, and stories of the rise and falls of the nations of the world, and he has given due consideration to their causes. He concludes that one of those causes was the affirmation and negation of *khudi* or self. The term "self" has been used simultaneously with the term *khudi*, ego, personality, and individual. It means self-realization and self-assertion which refine human personality, and help man in achieving God-gifted greatness[4]. Iqbāl invokes man to properly realize his self, and know it essentially as it deserved, and then he should attain the knowledge of God. To him, knowledge of God was dependent on the knowledge of *khudi* or self. Without the proper knowledge of self, it was not possible to have the due

---

[3] Yakob Masih, *The Hindu Religious Thought* (3000BC-200A.D) (Delhi: Motilal Baanargidass, 1983), p. 372.

[4] Nicholson. R.A., *Introduction to the Secrets of the Self: A Versified English Translation of Iqbal's Asrar-i- khudi* (London, 1978), pp. 36, 41.

knowledge of God. Furthermore, Iqbāl sees self as a real and pre-eminently significant entity which is the center of all our activities and actions. Therefore, he rejects all philosophical and religious schools of thought, which denied the reality of the self and regards it as a mere illusion of mind possessing no abiding reality of its own. This idea was influenced by the Platonic and Neo-Platonic philosophies which regarded the world as a mere illusion not worth striving for.

Iqbāl rejects all the pantheistic movements of thought, which believed that the highest objective and ideal of man is to lose his individual identity in the Absolute[5]. The concept of self-negation or its absorption into God began to consider weakness, laziness and inaction as fascinating things, and it holds a renunciation of the world, and escape from the struggle of life as a means of success and freedom. Iqbāl sees this conception as the main cause for the decline of Muslims. Thus, the moral and religious ideal of man, according to Iqbāl, is not self-negation, but it must be self-assertion or self-realization[6].

In his criticism of the phenomena of stagnation and backwardness of Muslim, Iqbāl elaborates that the self should face and strive with the universe in its development. Constant

---

[5] In his *AsrÉr-i –khudi*, Iqbāl asserts, "obviously this view of man and the universe is opposed to all forms of pantheistic *sufism* which regard absorption in a universal life or soul as the final aims and salvation of man". See Nicholson. R.A., *Introduction to the Secrets of the Self: A Versified English Translation of Iqbal's Asrar-i- khudi*, p.xviii.

[6] One can achieve this by becoming more and unique individual. Man is "not like that poor drop of water, which flows into the sea, and looses its individual existence, but his position is like a drop of water, which becomes a pearl in the sea". See Muĺammad Iqbāl, *The Reconstruction of Religious Thought in Islam* (Lahore: Sh. Muhammad Ashraf, 1982), p. 96. See also Abu Sayed Nuruddin, *Allama Iqbal's Attitude toward Sufism and His Unique Philosophy of Khudi- Self* (Bangladesh: Islamic Foundation Bangladesh, 1978), p. 36.

and creative activities and active participation in the affairs of the universe should be the goal of man's life. This goal of man, according to Iqbāl, is suit to his highest position as the vicegerent of God on earth. The development of the inner resources of his self enables him to develop the community at large when he becomes a master of his destiny and 'co-worker' with God in His planning of the universe. Clearly, Iqbāl introduces the dynamic theory of self as a revolutionary movement for reconstruction of the mystical thought in Islam, and this is a new approach in the history of Islamic mysticism. By his new approach, Iqbāl is strongly against sufis ideas of *waĺdah-al-wujËd* or pantheism, which holds that man, is completely absorbed by God. Rather, Iqbāl prefers man's separation instead of his complete union with God, because to him, God is God, and man is His creation. Iqbāl believes that servant –ship with God is the highest achievement of man.

In his rejection to the idea of self-negation and pantheism, Iqbāl is really concerned about the effect of the idea, which had been negative for the Islamic world. The effect was that Muslims of the world have grown up with an attitude of lost interest in action, renunciation of the world, and asceticism, which according to Iqbāl were against the original spirit of Islam. As a vicegerent of God, man has an active role to play in running the affairs of the universe through utilizing his creative faculties. God has made the whole creation subservient to man in order to enable him to perform his task as a vicegerent of God. Allah said,

> "And we subdued for thyself which are in the heavens and the earth all of them"[7]. "Do not see that God has subjected to your use all things in the heavens and on the earth and has made His

---

[7] Qur'an: al-baqarah, v.30

bounties flow to you in exceeding measures, seen and unseen"[8].

It means the entire universe has been created only for the service of man, so man should utilize it in a proper way. Iqbāl urges man to look at this gift of Allah as the proof for the greatness of human self, whereby when man becomes the servant as well as vicegerent of God, the entire universe becomes obedient and submissive to him. Everything in nature is subjected to man and he can empower them to steer and control his own destiny, the way he wants provided that he fortifies his self. Therefore, Iqbāl gives emphasis on the comprehensive power of the self.

Meanwhile, the concept of self-negation did not regard the comprehensive power of the self, and it thought the people to keep away from the universe and all in it, instead of subduing it. Iqbāl, on the other hand, believes that a renunciation of the world does not mean abandonment of the world, rather, Islam insists on subduing it; and self with its power gifted by God rules over everything of the universe. When Iqbāl presents this idea, it does not mean he is a materialist. He was rather a strong supporter and exponent of spiritualism[9]. He defines self as something spiritual, which cannot be developed without striving. For Iqbāl, self is an achievement, the fruit of constant, strenuous effort and struggle, both against the disruptive tendencies within man himself. According to Iqbāl,

"The life of the ego is a kind of tension caused by the ego invading the environment and the environment invading by the ego"[10].

---

[8] Qur'an: Luqman: 20

[9] This has been expressed by himself, "I am a Muslim, and by the grace of Allah, I shall die as a Muslim. In my opinion, the material interpretation of the history is absolutely wrong. I am a supporter of spiritualism". See Iqbāl, *Reconstruction*, p. 55

[10] Iqbāl, *Reconstruction*, 102.

Therefore, the living intimacy of the relationship between the individual and his environment should be preserved. Iqbāl sees the relationship between the individual and the universe as a dynamic process, whereby he holds that both man and the universe are incomplete and are undergoing growth and development. It is man who has to shape his own as well as the destiny of the universe.

The rise or fall of individuals and nations, according to Iqbāl, is due to strengthening or weakening of their self. If the individuals or nation directs their attention toward realizing, and affirming of self, they will become strong and could survive in power and greatness. And they will lose all the power and dignity as soon as they negate their self, and do not become aware of its weakness. Therefore, everything that strengthens self is good, and everything that weakens it is evil. Iqbāl asserts that we should strengthen the self, and bring it to perfection. Man should strive towards the achievement of a rich personality and come nearest to God[11].

According to Iqbāl, the life of self lies essentially in its will-attitudes, or, it is essential for man to have some ideas and purposes. To achieve this purpose, man naturally has desires in his heart. It is natural because life for us is synonymous with desires, longings, and yearnings. A man devoid of these is devoid of life, and the more we taste them, the more we ascend in the scale of life[12]. In *sufism*, this desire and longing is also called

---

[11] Though by nature man is self-contained center, he does not remain confined to himself, rather he proceeds forward in his life towards the most perfect individual, or the Absolute Ego, God. In his *Reconstruction*, Iqbāl beliefs that, "man as a self-contained centre, but he is not yet a complete individual. The greater his distance from God, the less is his of individuality. He who comes nearest to God is the completest person". See Nicholson. R.A., *Introduction to the Secrets of the Self: A Versified English Translation of Iqbal's Asrar-i- khudi*, p.xi.

[12] Ishrat Hasan Envar, *The Metaphysics of Iqbal* (Lahore: Sh. Muhammad Ashraf), p. 45.

shauq, yearning. The aim of the *sÉlik* (adapter) is actually to attain nearness to God. Iqbāl assumes these desires as a core of our personality. The self grows and expends into a strong and powerful personality by these desires and aspirations. Therefore, Iqbāl is opposed to the thought, which proposed us to get rid of desires.

In order to fortify the self and control the desires, Iqbāl lists several forces, which can strengthen the self or individual, for example, love, *faqr*, courage, tolerance, *kasb-i-ÍalÉl* (living on lawful earnings), and taking part in creative activities. Love has great importance to Iqbāl to fortify the self. In *sufism*, the highest form of love is called *ishg*, and Iqbāl uses this term in a large part in his philosophy. Love, for Iqbāl, carries a wide sense, whereby there are three stages of love; love of God, love of Prophet, and love of *shaikh* (spiritual teacher). So, love plays a dominant role, and it is the ideal and the goal of human life. By the term *faqr*, Iqbāl means that man should retain an inner attitude of detachment and superiority towards his material possessions while he engaged in the conquest of the universe[13]. This means man can guard himself against becoming a slave to the world or his worldly possessions. *Faqr* also can save man from an attitude of arrogance; it enables man to get rid of temptations. In relation to courage, Iqbāl refers to it as one of the greatest attributes possessed by man. If one looses courage, everything is lost. By the term courage, Iqbāl means both in physical and spiritual values. For tolerance, Iqbāl clearly states its significance of strengthening the human self. He says,

> "the principle of ego-sustaining deed is respect
> for the ego in myself as well as in others"[14].

---

[13] See Abdul Aleem Hilal, *Social Philosophy of Muhammad Iqbal: A Critical Study* (India: Adam Publishers and Distributors, 1995), p. 101.

[14] Iqbāl, *Reconstruction*, p. 113.

With regard to *kasb-i-ÍalÉl*, Iqbāl does not mean living on lawful earnings only, but he provides wider meaning, which is to prescribe for all human egos a life of active effort and struggle, and totally excludes all thoughts of self-renunciation. The last force of strengthening self, according to Iqbāl, is taking part in creative activities. So, he does not encourage passivity and imitation.

Meanwhile, the most important factor which weakens the self, in Iqbāl's opinion is asking or beggary. Iqbāl includes all things achieved without personal efforts in beggary[15]. For Iqbāl, this beggary would be a hindrance to development of the self as well as society. In short, Iqbāl believes that the self can only be reached to the highest point of development through performing self-sustaining deeds (for example love, *faqr*, courage, tolerance, *kasb-i –ÍalÉl)*, and by eliminating self-dissolving acts (for example beggary). Above all, this ideal of manhood can, indeed, be realized only through obedience to the law (*sharÊÑah*), and self-control, which is the highest form of self-hood.

THE RELATION OF SELF TO THE SOCIETY

Throughout the discussion of the self, Iqbāl focuses on its vitality and unity. He refutes the theories of Descartes, Hume and James due to their lack of essential nature and spiritual content. In case of Descartes, the soul is reduced to more passive observer of the body, and in case of Hume and James, the true character of the self is indefinable.

Iqbāl's approach to the self is a synthetic manner, combining both the theological and philosophical perspectives. He conceives self in both metaphysical and phenomenological parameters, thus, categorizes it into two aspects, "the appreciative self" and "the efficient self". The appreciative self reveals the self in its inner life

---

[15] Examples of beggary include the son who inherits his father's wealth, and the person who borrows his ideas from others.

and moves from the centre outwards, while the efficient self enters into relationship with space and forms the practical side of the self[16]. For Iqbāl, man should play an active role, constantly acting on and reacting purposefully to his environment. He stresses a life of strenuous activity and endeavor in the development of individuality. The self interacts with its material and cultural environment and utilizes them to realize the purpose of man's life as *'ibÉdullah* and *khalÊfullah*[17].

Talking about the growth and development of individuality, Iqbāl gives utmost importance to the concept of freedom. The freedom of the self, according to Iqbāl, is not absolute in its form; rather it is subject to his responsibility and accountability to God. It is self-organized and self-disciplined because it implies a great risk. Therefore, man should think of the consequences of his action. Iqbāl suggests that the inner urge of freedom must be controlled and guided by God under the teachings of Islam as a comprehensive code of life. Therefore, Iqbāl sees the activity of the self as a directive energy whereby man is free to act in this world under the direction of God for his living. This is parallel to the teachings of the *Qur'ān* as Allah said, "*To Him belong creation and direction*"[18]. For Iqbāl, freedom means that man is able to free himself from following his whims and turning himself to God, thus, full freedom means a total submission to God. The effect of a total submission to God is found in the establishment of a state based on the principle of the vicegerency of man and the sovereignty of God.

---

[16] Iqbāl, *Reconstruction*, p.76

[17] Iqbāl emphasized that the activity of man must be purposive and stated that, "it is not the origin of a thing that matters; it is the capacity, significance and the final reach of the emergent that matters". See Iqbāl, *Reconstruction*, p. 102.

[18] Qur'an, al-AÑraf, v. 54.

Regarding self as the basis of all the entire organization of life, Iqbāl claims that one has to first control his individual self, besides natural and social forces. He should be the master of his destiny both in individual and the social sphere for in his innermost being, man, as conceived by the *Qur'ān*, is an ascending spirit who is capable of changing the entire course of history.

In this world, the self is to act and react and disclose its capabilities and possibilities. The evolution of the self should be directed and commanded by God. Thus, Iqbāl refers the obedience and the love for Allah as the foremost conditions for the right growth of the self. Obedience, love, and discipline for Allah are viewed as the earlier stages of the self- evolution on the earth[19]. The last stage of the self-evolution, according to Iqbāl, is the vicegerent of Allah. It is the stage wherein the direction and will of Allah finds its all-inclusive and true fulfillment on the earth. Here, the self does not only illuminate his own personality, but radiates and transforms the whole social fabric of human beings for his own full and meaningful growth. It makes the self grow richer and brighter in the spatio-temporal world. At this level, it emerges the ideal and perfect man whom Iqbāl calls *insÉn-i-kÉmil* or *mu'min*

---

[19] According to Iqbāl, the human ego, in its development towards perfection, has to pass through three stages, obedience to the law, self-control, and Divine vicegerent. Obedience to the law and self-control, according to Iqbāl, play a great role in the development and fortification of the human ego, but he prefers to regard them as representing milestone in the upward march towards the goal of attaining the state of Perfect man. To an ego who is properly disciplined and suitably fortified, the first is represented by a phase where obedience to the law comes automatically. The ego has no conflicts to face so far as the law is concerned. Obedience to the law along with other favourable forces, tends to train the ego for the second evolutionary phase where it attains perfect self-control. Self-control, in its turn, prepares the ego for the third and the last stage of human development, for example, Divine vicegerent.

al -kÉmil[20]. Perfect man of Iqbāl is quite different from the perfect man of Ibn al 'ArabÊ and other pantheistic mystics of Islam. To Iqbāl, these mystics have upheld passivity and annihilation of the human self. For example, according to them, in order to attain perfection in life, an individual must merge himself in God, a belief, which resembles incarnation as expounded by Al-Mansur bin Al-Hallaj. As highlighted earlier, Iqbāl has totally repudiated this conception of pantheistic self-annihilation and advocated the necessity of self-assertion and self-realization. He has condemned all teachings and philosophies of life, which inspire man to self-annihilation and detachment from the world. For Iqbāl, perfect man played an active role as *ÑibÉdullah* and *khalÊfatullah* on earth and would transform the world in accordance with ideals set forth by Islam. He added that Muslims should gain power in order to supplement their spiritual potentials through practical capabilities. He once wrote,

> "Vision without power brings moral elevation, but could not establish a lasting culture. On the other hand, power without vision tends to be

---

[20] Some claim Iqbāl is influenced by Darwin and Nietzsche idea of the perfect man or superman. However, it should be noted that the perfect man of Iqbāl is different from that of Darwin (1809-882) and Nietzsche (1844-1900). According to Darwin, perfect man is one who survived physically in the rigid natural forces. He is not the man of the ideals and Divine values and man's personality is therefore, reduced to matter. Meanwhile, Nietzsche idea of superman is also totally different from Iqbāl. His concept is unconvincing as his free revolutionary thinking tends him to attribute man of the place of God. Besides, his denial of the existence of soul without body makes his superman a materialist whose entire development is physical.

destructive and inhuman. Human development
needs a combination of both"[21].

The self, according to Iqbāl, cannot grow in isolation and
solitude. In this regard, the life of the individual depends upon its
having established some connections with an objective reality, the
world, the community, or society. Here, I would like to elaborate
further on the questions closely related to the development of
self or individuality. For example, what position is assigned
to an individual in a society by Iqbāl? Is the development of
individuality an end in itself, or a means to some other end? Iqbāl's
response to these questions is different from the views of Kant,
Nietsche and Bergson, who attach the highest value to the freedom
of the individual. Iqbāl is also different from Hegel and Karl
Marx, who consider the society or state as a super entity whose
strength and integrity are far more important than the rights of
the individual. Iqbāl sees society as a must for the proper growth
and development of human self and it is only in society that man
can achieve self-realization and fulfills his missions. According
to Iqbāl, an individual can realize his self only within a society.
The individual's personality must take a social role and devote
itself to serving society. This does not at all mean the loss of his
individuality. On the contrary, the social path enables personality
to realize itself.

Iqbāl has recognized the relative importance of the individual
and society in his two Persian works we mentioned earlier, *AsrÉr-
i-khudi* (*The Secrets of the Self*) and *Rumuz-i -Bekhudi* (*The
Mysteries of Selflessness*). *The Secrets of the Self* deals with the
philosophy of the self or individual personality, and is intended
to guide the individual, whereas *The Mysteries of the Selflessness*

---

[21] Quoted in Mahmoud Esmail Nia, "Iqbal as a Social Reformer", paper
represented in *International Conference of Muhammad Iqbal and the
Asian Renaissance*, Kuala Lumpur, 3-5th June 1997, p 13.

deals with the philosophy of society, and is meant to guide the individual in relation to his society. Iqbāl has discussed the nature of mutual relationship between the individual and the cultural life of the society. It is society wherein man lives, moves, and exists[22]. In other words, man depends on society; if he is alone, he becomes weak and powerless, and his energies are scattered, and his aims become narrow, diffuse and indefinite. Thus, according to Iqbāl, the personal self can develop only in association with other selves and not in isolation. The self must adjust its social activities to the common good of society, and must not limit its vision to any form of personal profit at the expense of the common good. The adjustment of personal activity to social good is also beneficial to the self itself, because by this way only that it can achieve its highest possibilities. This is exactly in accordance with *Qur'anic* teaching *"And hold fast, all together, by the Rope, which God stretches out for you, and be not divided among yourself"* (111: 103).

According to Iqbāl, a harmonious working of the individual and society produces a durable human civilization, which in turn, fulfills the purpose of God. Both complement and supplement each other in their common struggle to achieve a good civilization. In other words, the individual is the internal and the society is the external manifestation of human civilization. For Iqbāl, there is a necessary relationship between the individual and the society and both contribute mutually to each other's development. The society helps the individual to discipline himself and to realize the best in him, while individuals gifted with the vision of high ideals, help

---

[22] Iqbāl says, "It is the active and living memberships of a vital community that confers on him a sense of power and makes him conscious of great collective purposes which deeper and widen the scope for the growth of his individual self". See Bang-i- Dara, 210. Quoted in K.G Saiyidain, *Iqbal's Educational Philosophy* (8th ed) (Lahore: Sh. Muhammad Ashraf, 1977), p.56.

society to develop. Iqbāl acknowledges that the attachment to a society is a blessing for the individual, because it is in society where individuals develop their personalities, and attain their perfection. He believed that individuals are the basic units of society, and a society is constituted and organized through individuals.

Iqbāl's concept of society is not narrow and parochial. According to him, it is not racial or geographical unity which can form the right basis of people's coherence. It is the unity of beliefs and purposes which cement a collection of individuals into a genuine human society. Thus, Iqbāl is strongly opposed to the prejudices of race and color as well as narrow nationalism because they are obstructions in the path of evolving a broad humanitarian outlook. It is, therefore, important to draw a clear distinction between the nationalism subordinated to the higher goal of the unity of mankind, as preached by Iqbāl, and unbridled nationalism, as practiced by the West which has invariably resulted in conflicts among nations all over the world. Iqbāl's plan of building a universal society started from Islam because of its administrative and social convenience. Since Islam vehemently opposes the idea of racial superiority, which is the greatest obstacle to international integration, he finds Islam the most suitable starting point for a better social order. Thus, it is very clear to point out that Iqbāl looks at the function of religion in the life of an individual and of the society, which gives birth to human culture and civilization.

Iqbāl has lied down some essential requirements for an ideal Muslim society. The most important requirement is that it must be based on the faith in the unity of God, *TawÍÊd*. For him, *tawÍÊd* is the soul of society because it generates unity of thought and unity of action in individuals who are bound together by society. Faith in prophethood or inspired leadership provides the second important corner-stone for the structure of the ideal Muslim society. He emphasizes the strength and the unity of the Muslim society are based on the adherence to the book of God and the practice of the Prophet (p.b.u.h). Thirdly, the very existence of the Muslim society is indebted to a code of law, which is provided through the Qur'anic law. Iqbāl hold that the Muslim society is impossible to exist without being governed by the Qur'anic law, and he identifies Muslims' failure to abide by the Qur'anic law as the primary cause for their decline. On the other hand, abiding by the Qur'anic law matures a society and helps it builds its character. Iqbāl calls the Qur'anic law as the code of power, which gives its followers the sinews of steel and stands them in very good stead. Its polishing turns a stone into a mirror and cleans the iron of all its rust[23]. Iqbāl has strongly advocated the reinterpretation of the Qur'anic law to meet the challenges of the changing times without compromising on the basic principles. Besides a code of law, an ideal society also needs a common centre for all its cultural and social activities. Iqbāl emphasizes that the unity of a society emanates from this very centre, and its existence can become strong by the strength of its centre. For the Muslims, this centre is provided by the *ka`bah* in Mecca. It helps in maintaining unity of the Muslims and promotes their integration as a religious community through a pilgrimage assembly once in a year. The next requirement for an ideal society is that it must have a goal towards which the whole community should strive. For Muslims, the objective is the preservation and propagation of the principle of *tawÍÊd*. Furthermore, the society must gain supremacy over the forces of nature. Every individual must acquire mastery over his environment by developing the study of science. The West owes its supremacy to its development of physical resources and study of natural phenomena, and one of the main causes of Eastern decadence is the neglect of science which has led to political and economic disintegration. The history of the Arabs shows the dire consequences resulting from a neglect

---

[23] Iqbāl, *Kulliyyat-i-Iqbal* (Lahore: Sh. Ghulam Ali and Sons, 1972), p. 127. Quoted in Muhammad Ashraf Chaudhri, *The Muslim Ummah and Iqbal* (Pakistan: Institute of Historical and Cultural Research, 1994), p. 129.

of science by the people. During the heyday of their progress, the Arabs led the people of the world in the study and civilization of science. However, when the Arabs came under the influence of pseudo-mystics and began neglecting the sciences, they soon lost the prominent position they had attained in the world. Iqbāl added that the societal or collective self must be developed in the same way as the individual self is developed. Last but not least, he gives emphasis on the importance of safeguarding maternity for the sake of preservation of the society. The real wealth of society, according to Iqbāl, consists in nothing but the virtue of children and children's children. Therefore, maternity must be honoured.

Clearly, Iqbāl's philosophy of self has not only provided a complete scheme for the development of individuals but also has prescribed the essentials of the society, which will help the development of the individual and, on the other hand, provide the best scope for the creative unfolding of man's individuality.

CONCLUSION

In conclusion, Iqbāl is strongly opposed to the doctrine of self-negation by practical grounds. He traces the connection between this doctrine and the decadence, which characterized all Eastern people in general and Muslim people in particular. By analyzing and criticizing this doctrine, which had influenced intellectuals and psychological life of all Eastern people, Iqbāl came forth to challenge the doctrine by proclaiming that life is real and not a mere illusion. Based on his idea of self-affirmation, Iqbāl made an attempt to interpret the reality of life in terms of human will and action. Since man, according to Iqbāl, is the supreme creation of God, therefore, he must realize his inherent ability, power and possibilities for the progress of society and for the perfection of his own personality. As a whole, Iqbāl does not only preach self-affirmation by individuals, but his idea also prescribes suppression of preserve individualism, which precludes any collective and concerted action.

BIBLIOGRAPHY

1. Muĺammad Iqbāl, *The Reconstruction of Religious Thought in Islam* (Lahore: Sh. Muhammad Ashraf, 1982).
2. Abu Sayed Nuruddin, *Allama Iqbal's Attitude toward Sufism and His Unique Philosophy of Khudi-Self* (Bangladesh: Islamic Foundation Bangladesh, 1978).
3. Nicholson R. A, *Introduction to the Secrets of the Self: A Versified English Translation of Iqbal's Asrar-i -Khudi* (Lahore, 1978).
4. Ishrat Hasan Envar, *The Metaphysics of Iqbal* (Lahore: Sh. Muhammad Ashraf, 1991).
5. Abdul Aleem Hilal, *Social Philosophy of Muhammad Iqbal: A Critical Study* (India: Adam Publishers and Distributors, 1995).
6. K.G. Saiyidain, *Iqbal's Educational Philosophy* (Lahore: Sh. Muhammad Ashraf, 3rd edition, 1945).
7. Yakub Masih, *The Hindu Religious Thought* (3000 BC-200 A.D) (Delhi: Motilal Banarsidass, 1983).
8. Asif Iqbal Khan, *Some Aspects of Iqbal's Thought* (Pakistan: Islamic Book Service, 1977).
9. Sayed Abdul Vahid, *Iqbal: His Art and Thought* (Lahore: Sh. Muhammad Ashraf, 1848).
10. Eminent Scholars Essays, *Iqbal as a Thinker* (Lahore: Sh. Muhammad Ashraf, 1991).
11. Mahmoud Esmail Nia, "Iqbal as a Social Reformer" in *International Conference of Muhammad Iqbal and the*

Asian Renaissance (Kuala Lumpur: Conference Paper, 3-5th June 1997).

12. Muhammad Ashraf Chaudhri, *The Muslim Ummah and Iqbal* (Pakistan: Institute of Historical and Cultural Research, 1994).

WORLDVIEW AND HUMAN DEVELOPMENT IN SECULAR AND ISLAMIC FRAMEWORK

Hafas Furqani
&
Zakariya Bin Man

IntroductionAny system of thought is founded on a specific worldview which provides the basis and objectives as well as a set of axioms and principles on which that system operates. In addition, a system of thought should always associate with worldview that initiates changes and development of that particular system. Direction, changes or progress in any system of thought is defined by its worldview as Khaliq (1992: 308) rightly observes that "science, necessarily needs metaphysical outlook that will provide significant pointers to the direction in which scientific progress should advance." The worldview will eventually culminate in institutions that capture the spirit and the message of foundational philosophy and bring them into certain direction. Nasr (1986) in this regard rightly asserts that:

> The elaboration and in certain instances construction of the omnipotent of philosophy, *weltanschauung,* or more generally the spiritual

content of a belief system 'preceded' the emergence of the institutions or organizational expressions which were the bearers of the message and implements of the objectives of those original ideas. Religious law, meanwhile, has always acted as the guiding criterion for the explication of the original ideas and the delineation of the activities of the institutions which emanated from those ideas.

At the intellectual level, the worldview within which we perceive 'reality' has immense impact not only on our theoretical understanding of reality, but also on practical consequences (Golshani: 2000; Swidler: 2002). At the theoretical level, the worldview and philosophical presumptions influence the scientist in his theory-making or choice of theories. As for the practical dimension, the worldview influences the formation of system of thought and cultural traditions of scientist.

Difference in worldview, consequently, leads to different conclusion on certain issues or object of study. While the object of study might be similar, the perspectives to look it and conclusion derived might be different. Let take the science of Economics for example, while the behaviour of human being is the subject matter of economics (capitalism or Islamic), the notion of economic man, his behaviour in making actions and decisions, his goals to be achieved as well as the concept of his progress and development are differ from one to another. Each system of thought will provide answers based on their ontological argument and particular worldview that lead to different schools of thought.

This difference is the main impetus for us to investigate in this paper. The main thesis is that, the ontological position, i.e., worldview implicates to certain notions on the nature of human being (in this case economic man), his behaviour, goals as well as his development. The study will explore first the implication of worldview on the construction of 'economic man' in the case of conventional economics and 'Islamic man' in the case of Islamic economics. Then, we will also investigate the implication of worldview in conceiving the notion of human development and progress.

Worldview and The conception of economic man

Modern economics is preceded by what Schumpeter (1954) and Heilbroner (1988) call a "vision" or an "ideology" which is constructed from the secularist-materialist worldview of Western civilization.[24] That worldview, which is constructed from the Western society's experience, plays a role in conceiving the substance of modern economics as Spengler (1980: xiii) observes "the content of economic thought was not initially independent of the socio-physical parameters of the society within which it developed, nor did it ever become completely independent even in modern times." He further contends "economic science is essentially a product of European civilization with some of its origin dating back to the Greco-Roman and medieval worlds" (p. xii). Therefore, there is an ontological bias of economics which will not make it as universal economics to understand the whole type of society or the whole human being as implied by Heilbroner (1999: 310) in his classic book *The Worldly Philosopers* that contemporary economics "is not a science of society, its purpose is to help us better understand the capitalist setting in which we will most likely have to shape our collective destiny for the

---

[24] Heilbroner (1988) sees ideology as a part of economics since its "motivations are not only powerful, inescapable, but legitimate".

foreseeable future."[25] Modern economics is a special economics with limited scope to explain the behavior of human being based on several assumptions built upon the Western's worldview and shaped by western society's experience.

Those assumptions gradually become postulates and 'untestable' dogma in economics. The worldview of materialism and secularism considers human behavior in a materialistic perspective by merely concerned on self-material satisfaction and secularist perspective by detaching individual from religion. Any religious/spiritual insight is considered irrelevant. The materialist and secular view of the ultimate nature of human being believes that human action is motivated merely by the materialistic side of human being. His action is basically a response of his natural urge to increase the self-utility and to satisfy all his desire. Human being also will avoid any pain that will reduce his utility.

In this effort to conceive the nature of economic man, the metaphysic is removed and the role of religion is eliminated. Scientific methods require source of knowledge from a verifiable sources and not a dogmatic or mythological doctrine. They have found the alternative of God in the nature. The nature is claimed to be running based on certain fixed and harmoneous law and this "law of nature" is the ultimate source of knowledge that could explain realities, which is not only in physical realities of the universe but also in the microcosmic nature of human being. The beauty of this law is in its consistency and harmony so that it can predict and forecast well the future.

---

[25] The statement reflects aspirations underlying the theories put together over nearly 200 years by the great economic thinkers that he reviews: Adam Smith, David Ricardo, Thomas Malthus, John Stuart Mill, Karl Marx, Alfred Marshall, Thorstein Veblen, John Maynard Keynes, and Joseph Schumpeter. Their legacy is a quest for "socially as well as economically successful capitalisms" (Baghirathan et al., 2004).

The successful development of science of physics, in the post renaissance, has inspired other branch of sciences to adopt their approaches as well as assumptions. Thomas Hobbes (1588-1679) in his *Leviathan* has initiated modern ethical theory to explain the psychology of man that is based on "law of nature". Inspired by the Galilean natural science, he conceives man as a complex system of particles in motion and derives the tendency of "self preservation" as the principle of the law of ethics. Hobbes regarded the preservation of life as the paramount goal of human action, the idea that has led to the emergence of ethical philosophies of naturalism, cultural relativism, and subjectivism respectively. Adam Smith (1732-1790) has refined utilitarian ethics of 'self preservation', constructed by Locke, and applied utilitarian ethics to economic theory. He is promoting individual self-interest behavior to be the foundation of capitalism and the basis of economic analysis (Abelson and Nielsen, 2006).

Later on, utility maximization, individual rationality and self-interest become the primary assumptions in economic capitalism. Those assumptions, they argue, are very close to the fact (the reality as it is) and could properly explain the behavior of economic man. With the triumph of methodological positivism in economics, economic man behavior should be as close as possible to the fact. Economics is not interested in explaining of what "ought to be" where value should be separated from facts. *Homo economicus* (with the assumptions that we will explain in part 3) is conceived as the ultimate nature of human being that perfectly represents the actual view of the nature of man as he "is".

As a positive science, economics is interested in describing the fact as 'it is' and not as 'ought to be'. Friedman (1953) as the main opponent of positive economics emphasizes the goal of mainstream economics as being the logistics for greater precision in economic predictions based on the view of the world as 'is', not as it 'ought' to be.

The nature of economic agent, that is going to be conceived, therefore must be constant so that his action can be "predicted". For that reason, an economic theory must be free from any particular set of value judgments or any philosophical or psychological framework as they will change the behavioral pattern thus the prediction could be misleading (Drakoupoulos, 1997). The scientific nature of discipline requires economic theories to be the statements, propositions or models about patterns of human behavior that occur expectedly under certain circumstances (which are assumed to be fixed). The models and theories then will be utilized to sort out and understand the complexities of economic behavior and can be used as the guidance in economic analysis (Sexton, 2006: 8).

Such notion of economic agent who is driven by self-interest is argued to follow the "moral equivalent of the force of gravity in nature" (Myers, 1983, 4). The nature of human being in this regard is reduced to be an autonomous/atomistic individual in all his activities where he measures value at the level of personal impulses, desires and preferences (Ryan, 2003: 249). Such cconception according to Davis (2003: 17) is the result of the "methodological individualism" applied by mainstream economics. Methodological individualism is a doctrine within which "all explanations of social phenomena have to be couched in terms of statements about individuals. . . a refusal to examine the institutional or other forces which are involved in the molding of individual preferences and purposes" (Hodgson, 1988: 53–56). It is ". . . usually associated with the reductionism claim that all theories of Social Science are reducible to theories of individual human action" (Wolozin, 2001: 48). Methodological individualism believes that social structure is influenced by individuals and the individuals in various fundamental respects are not influenced by social structures (Davis, 2003: 128).

Therefore, the main purpose of this generic and simplistic behavior of homo economicus is not in explaining the "whole truth" of economic agent as it is and as it should be, but that because of its purported usefulness in generating successful predictions and leads to some verifiable conclusions of a theory that can easily be empirically tested and possibly rejected in the scientific research. Friedman (1935: 21) again admits this by saying that "to be important . . . a hypothesis must be descriptively false in its assumptions". By this he meant that we should treat economic actors "as if" they were guided perfectly by those motives of 'maximizing behavior' that would produce the results that the theory will successfully predict (though such behavior might not be correct morally or unable to explain the whole truth). Such assumption is necessary to make possible the mathematical modeling of economic problems (Samuelson, 1952). The statement that could be traced back to John Locke (1632-1704) who believes in a deductive method in which specific rules of conduct are derived "from self-evident propositions, by necessary consequences as incontestable as those in mathematics" (Abelson and Nielson, 2006: 407).

The conventional economists in this regard are not interested in the realism of the assumptions but only about its predictive value. *Homo economicus* is a construct or abstraction that is useful for getting definite theoretical results, a construct that is used largely because of its consistency with the deductive mathematical models. This generic assumption of *homo economicus* behavior is then serviceable for a variety of types of agents, firms, individuals, government agencies, unions, clubs, organizations, and so on where analysis is being made on this self-interest assumption (Davis, 2003: 96; Tomer, 2001: 282).

Through out the history of economic discourse, the concept of *homo economicus* as in the above description has invited numerous critics from various scholars especially on its 'unrealistic' assumptions and its 'detachment of ethics'. Scholars, such as Amartya Sen (1990: 9) observes that such this concept of man will make economics as an 'unproductive science'. Kirzner

(1976: 53), likewise, rejects this idea by arguing that such view of human nature in economics instead of making it a credible science leads to a 'narrow' scope of economics since a *homo economicus* is endowed with only one aspect of human nature, that of greed (self interest), to be the main postulate, which subsequently we can see the whole body of economic theory as the extended exposition of the consequences of this greed.

If we scrutinize further the reason why conventional economics has such narrow conception of economic agent, is actually because they have a very 'narrow' worldview that only acknowledge 'narrow' realities which is sensible materialism.

Islamic Worldview and the Conception of Islamic Man

The subject matter of Islamic economics as a discipline, for some scholars, is also the behavior of human being in allocating the resources and answering the economic problems. Arif (1985), for example, defines Islamic economics as "the study of Muslim's behaviour who organizes the resources, which are a trust, to achieve *falāh*." M.A. Choudhury (1986: 4) defines Islamic economic as "the sum total of historical, empirical, and theoretical studies that analyze the human and the societal wants in the light of an integrated Islamic value system." Khurshid Ahmad (1992:19) defines Islamic economics as "a systematic effort to try to understand the economic problem and man's behaviour in relation to the problem from an Islamic perspective." Naqvi (1994: 20) defines Islamic economics as "a study of the representative Muslim's behaviour in a modern Muslim society." And Kahf (2003) defines Islamic economics as "the study of economic behaviour of men and women, as individual economic agents, and as communities and collective entities."

Since the subject matter is the behavior of human being, then the presence of an economic agent in an Islamic framework who will apply Islamic principles in economics is a necessity. Mannan

(1984: 56) writes *homo Islamicus* is "a must for the successful operation of the Islamic socio-economic system." Without *homo Islamicus*, Islamic socio-economic framework can not be properly implemented.

The concept of human behavior in Islamic economics is different to the concept of human behavior in conventional economics as the notion of the objective of Islamic economics as well as the 'expected' behavior of human being to achieve that objective is different. The differences arise due to the ontological differences in economic vision (ie., worldview).

Conventional economics is constructed from the secular worldview that would eliminate any insight from divine revelation (religion). The perspective on the nature of man is purely come from philosophical speculation of reasoning or accumulated man life experience. *Homo economicus* is constructed from that worldview. [26] *Homo Islamicus*, who will be the economic agent in Islamic economic analysis, is constructed from the Islamic worldview of how Islam perceives the nature of human being. The ultimate source of Islamic worldview is the revelation (i.e., the

---

[26] This is not surprising since science and scientific activities are the result of specific ontology which relates the scientific endeavor of the individual to his environment and furnishes their motivational basis. Therefore, knowledge in Islam is not neutral as commonly argued in western epistemology (Furqani, 2006). Al-Attas (1993: 133) asserts "It seems to be important to emphasize that knowledge is not neutral, and can indeed be infused with a nature and content that masquerades as knowledge. Yet it is in fact, taken as a whole, not true knowledge but its interpretation through the prism, as it were, the world-view, the intellectual vision and psychological perception of the civilization that now plays the key role in its formulation and dissemination. What is formulated and disseminated is knowledge infused with the character and personality of that civilization – knowledge presented and conveyed as knowledge in that guise to subtly fused together with the real so that others take it unaware *in toto* to be the real knowledge *perse*".

Qur'an and Sunnah) where God, who has created human being, has revealed of where he come from, why he has been created, and what is his destiny in earthly life.

Islamic worldview perceives reality not like the West, devoid of the Divine. Al-Attas (1993) notes the meaning of worldview in Islam as *ru'yat al-Islām li al-wujūd* and not *nazrat al-Islām li al-kawn*. A Worldview in Islam is not merely the mind's view of the physical world and of man's historical, social, political and cultural involvement in it (as the latter phrase denotes). It is beyond that. Worldview in Islam is the way Islam looks at the existences (*al-wujūd*) of God, human-beings and the total universe, and not the way Islam looks at merely the physical universe (*al-kawn*), which usually leads to God-negation metaphysics and a purely materialistic view of reality. The Islamic worldview links inseparably the life in this world (*al-dunya*) with the life in the hereafter (*al-akhirah*). The Islamic worldview, in the word of Sayyid Qutb (1991: 1) aims at explaining human being with the 'real' realities that confront him which is the reality of the Creator and the created (which include the universe, life and man), the nature of relationship of these realities and their mutual interconnection.

In Islamic worldview, the ultimate reality is God while the others are only manifestation of this reality. Therefore, the ultimate objective in Islamic economics is not man as in conventional. Izutsu (2002: 76), in his *God and Man in the Qur'an*, observes that ontologically, the Qur'anic world is most evidently *theocentric* where God stands in the very centre of the world of being and all other things are His creatures and are as such inferior to Him in the hierarchy of being.

This unique worldview then is going to be adopted, applied and integrated in the conception of Islamic economic agent that will be broaden his nature, responsibility and objective, rather than merely an individual agent equipped with self-interest, motivated merely by the materialistic side of the human being, and has a vision of merely to this temporary life as in conventional economics. Islamic man has a spiritual-transcendental dimension. His self-interested behavior will not be pursued at the expense of social interest or against regulations set up by God. His motivation is not only to increase his own utility and valued by the material progress but also others, utility and valued beyond materialist reward. His behavior is consciously targeted to reach happiness in this world and the world after. He will submit to God in all his economic pursuits. Islamic economics, model and theory, will not restrict man's vision to his existence in this world without any thought of the hereafter.

Islamic economics will not emphasize only one side of behavior as conventional did. But see him as a complete creature, has a potential to be a perfect human being (*al-insan al-kamil*). The nature of human is broadened in Islamic perspective as not to be the physical being with the goal of materialism *perse*. Human being is a physical-intellectual-spiritual being as envisaged in the following verses. His needs are broader to include physical, moral, intellectual and spiritual.

> "Such is He: the All-Knower of the unseen and the seen, the All-Mighty, the Most Merciful. Who made everything He has created good and He began the creation of man from clay. Then He made his offspring from semen of despised water (male and female sexual discharge). Then He fashioned him in due proportion, and breathed into him the soul (created by Allah for that person); and he give you hearing (ears), sight (eyes) and hearts. Little is the thanks you give." (Al-Sajadah, 32, 6-9).

Human Progress and Development in Islamic and Secular Framework

The characteristics of economic man as being outlined in the above explanations will be the basis in outlining the criteria of human achievement, progress and development. In conventional economics, the ability of economic man to fulfill and realize the characteristics of individual's rationality, self-interest and ethics externality of religion and social values is the main criteria for human development and progress. The economic indicator is usually structured and indexed based on the calculation of material. The basic assumption is that the higher a person can achieve percapita income, the more welfare he gets, and therefore he achives progress. Spiritual achievement and progress is not included in this calculation. It is not only because spirituality is an abstract concept which cannot be measured, but also because, in the modern context, spirituality become less significant.

Modern society in a secular tradition consider wealth material achievement as the primary goal in his life. The role of religion in modern society has been decreasing as a result of modernization which is characterized by industrialization, urbanization, individualization, rationalization, and pluralization (Pollack, 2008: 1).

At the axiological level, the ethical notions of what is good or bad, right or wrong is also defined in accordance to what extent they are able to achieve the purposes. Since the objective is measured in the form of materialism, the more we can achieve material satisfaction (wealth) is better and thereby the more we progress and success.

Individual freedom and satisfaction is the basis for his progress and development. This concept, in the Western intellectual tradition, was influenced by the renaissance and post-renaissance notion of man as being in revolt against the doctrine of religion. Freedom is conceived as freedom *to do* or *to act* in a real freedom of choice of individuals not in the cage of religious doctrine. In this perspective, freedom could be meant as free to choose of God and evil, or right and wrong, as long as they are in line with individuals, preferences, and their own will and consciousness. Therefore, sometime freedom could be understood in terms of liberation from religious worldview, or liberation of one self from the traditional ethical dogma.

In Islam, freedom and progress is understood differently. Freedom and therefore progress mean to choose God in preference of evil, to choose virtues in preference of vice, or in the word of Muhammad Iqbal, it is the self "surrender to the moral ideals" that could lead him into a meaningful place and function in relation to the whole of Reality surrounded him in his life (Bakar, 1997: 65). [27] That is the real progress and development in Islam. In the case of Islamic economics, the ability of individual to realize the Islamic rationality, multiple-interests, and to incorporate Islamic ethics in all his economic actions are the criteria for progress and development.

It is true that man is endowed with freedom of the possibility of doing or not doing. He is a unique creation as he is granted a "free will" to select and choose. He then could act voluntarily and none force him except his own consciousness. But Islam also teaches that all decisions made and actions taken have values, none are useless and all will be valued by God. Therefore, Islam requires a 'purposeful' action and not a 'meaningless' one. The purposeful action is the action that attempts to realize the purpose of Divine's

---

[27] Therefore, those who have chosen vice over good, evil over God, should "liberate" him self as he has been confined in the immoral cage and meaningless place. They have been moved far away from the ultimate meaning and destiny of his creation. Islam has equipped mankind with the moral and spiritual teachings that could help in this liberation, reviving the spiritual basis of life and rediscovering the ultimate meaning and destiny of his life. The development and progress is defined in this liberation.

will and patterns, i.e., the realization of obligations towards God, nature and other humans (Nasr, 1981: 18). Individual is said to have progress if he is able to do that. The concept of economic man as understood in conventional economics is not in line with Islam, since it envisages complete freedom for human existence without considering the source, and also the end, of his existence which make his life meaningless.

Islam clearly teaches that no progress can be achieved gained through flight from or rebellion against the principle which is the ontological source of human existence and which determines ourselves. Humans are in Islamic perspective created in the 'image of God' and are also 'God's vicegerent' *(khalifah)* on earth. Individual as well as society's progress and development lies, in fact, in surrender to the divine will and in purifying oneself inwardly to an ever greater degree so as to become liberated from all external conditions, including those of the carnal soul *(nafs)*, which press upon and limit one's freedom. In this regard, religion will locate them within a sacred and cosmic frame of reference. Therefore, the form of freedom in Islam is the freedom *to be*. The freedom 'to do' and 'to act', in the absence of guidance of the freedom 'to be', i.e., by rebelling against our own ontological principle is actually not freedom but to enslave our self to another entity which is the *hawa* or *nafs*. By this time, humans are neither free nor progress and indeed they are caught and limit themselves in the cage of another ontological principle which is *materialism* or *desire (taghut or hawa)*.

Human freedom is always respected in Islamic tradition but in the view of "the necessity to conform to the Divine will which rules over both the cosmos and human society and which alone can prevent men from becoming imprisoned in the narrow confines of their own passions" (Nasr, 1981: 20). Freedom never meant individualism that would detach individual from the cosmic structure, but rather to penetrate and integrate the individual into the centre, the absolute and the higher reality. Freedom is exercised within certain 'protective code' that would bind from any transgressions. The sufi's understanding of freedom according to Nasr (1981: 21) means "ultimately deliverance (*najat*) from all bondage and an experience of the world of the Spirit where alone freedom in its real sense is to be found." In this regard, soul becomes detached from all external factors and also from passionate attachments and the desires and needs. Human being in this regard is said to have progress if he is able to release himself from being slave to his *nafs* (limited interest), *hawa* (unguided desires), or *taghut* (another God), and therefore he moves into the direction of controlling his own interest in order to respect and pursue other's interests, controlling his *hawa* so that he will not exploit others' interests for the sake satisfaction of his own interest.

The secular and material tradition of the west might see the Islamic concept of human development as limitations imposed to human freedom and therefore will limit his development. Such total submission to the God, in secular framework, is ethically incorrect as it implies force, unconscious action, totalitarianism and does not entail freedom for human being. Al-Attas, however, argues that this *submission* to God does not entail loss of 'freedom' for human being since freedom is in fact means *to act as his true nature demand*. The *submission* in the meaning of *din* is in fact a *natural inclination (fitrah)* of human being as before his existence as a physical human being he has recognized his Creator and Cherisher and Sustainer; "*When thy Lord drew forth from the Children of Adam – from their loins – their descendents, and made them testify concerning themselves (saying): 'Am I not your Lord?' – they said: 'Yea! We do testify!* (Al-Mu'minun, 23: 12-14)" The statement has sealed a Covenant with God (*mithaq*) that implies recognition of human being of their ultimate destiny by acknowledging and confirming the covenant and then promise to willingly submit to God. *Fitrah* in this regard is also meant moral innate endowed by the Creator to human being so that he is able to recognize what is good and beautiful and what is bad and morally ugly. He has been granted a conscience that registers right and wrong and a mind that has the ability to reason (Wahid, 2004: 13). This constitutes the second criteria of progress and development. Human being achieves progress and development if he is able to put himself back to his *fitrah* as an *'abd* of his Lord, commit to his primordial covenant with God, commit to the *din* and *Islam,* and manage to do His commands and to avoid His prohibitions.

Progress in Islam is to return to the original spirit by means of sincere submission (*Islam*) to God's Will and obedience to His regulations, fulfilling the obligations toward God, nature and human being, as being enacted and regulated by the *din.* In the ethical dimension, the sincerity to return to the condition of genuine Islam (*fitrah*) is viewed as real development and progress of human self. It is a sacred character bestowed upon human life which in turn makes possible a greater inner freedom (Nasr, 1981: 18). Unwilling submission, on the other hand, when he has been created, is a form of betrayal, arrogance, disobedience, rebellion, unbelief, immoral (*kufr*) and therefore a form of retreat/decline. Al-Attas (1993: 85) also notes that *kufr* also can be in the form of not real submission as one prefers to submit to his own obstinate way, a way that neither approved nor revealed and commanded by

God.[28] Therefore, progress is not merely by increasing our own self interest and maximizes our material prosperity as in secular teaching. Islam considers those achievements as progress only if they are pursued in line with Islamic principle.

The exercise of freedom in this framework (I.e., rules and obligations) opens the possibilities of human being to achieve highest moral achievement which is *taqwa*. *Taqwa* is the all composite of ethics in Islam and the highest form of progress and development. *Taqwa* is the fear of God which springs from the heart and expresses itself in righteous deeds. Fazlur Rahman sees the implication of *taqwa* when ethics will converge into any system and practice that we have in life of politics, economics or law. The loss of *taqwa* in the ethical system might lead to other evil consequences to emerge such as the social justice is eliminated, etc.

---

[28] Al-Attas (1993: 85) further adds that man's covenant with God (*al-mitsaq*) "is of an essential nature; it is the starting point in the Islamic concept of religion, and is the dominant element in all other Islamic concept of religion bound up with it, such as those of freedom and responsibility, of justice, of knowledge, of virtue, of brotherhood; of the role and character of the individual and the society and of their mutual identity in the framework of the state and of collective life". Al-Faruqi (1992: 81) explains that the semithic religion (jews and Chrisitian) has this covenant wherein man is to serve God and they are also aware of the opposite of not serving God. Judaism however has altered the covenant into one directional commitment on the part of God to favor the Jews regardless of their piety or righteousness, and for the Christians, this is a unilateral commitment of God to love and ransom His partner (i.e., man) even through he sins against God. Islam has maintained that the covenant gives obligation to both parties, the one to serve and the other to reward; and to privileges to both parties, the one to defy and not serve, and the other to punish.

CONCLUDING REMARKS

Conventional economics has characterized economic man as individualistic, utility-maximizer, rational man, and his treatment of ethics as exogenous variable. There are many critics currently to a narrow concept of economic man that treat human being as a 'half person', having narrow behavior by not considering social and spiritual motivation. Such conception of economic agent emerged because of the secularist-materialist worldview that will not allow any insight from revelation in human sphere. The concept of "realities" has been narrowly defined into sensible and material realities. This worldview promotes reductionism that tends to reduce realities into a physical reality only. In economics, the concept is applied by using methodological individualism that reduces man as an atomistic individual, and considers all explanations of social phenomena have to be couched in terms of statements about individuals. The ethics, religious spirituality become an exogonous variables that do not influence individual behavior directly and are irrelevant, unless that ethics or religious spirituality could increase his own utility.

This 'narrow' worldview is lack of rigorous standards for conceiving the true individuals in proper sense. Human being should be treated as a real individual whereby all his attitude and behaviour is taken into consideration. The behavioral assumption of homo economicus is lack of 'individuation criteria', where one cannot differentiate many-person individuals and single-person individuals since all individuals are assumed to have single behavior (Davis, 2003: 43). A comprehensive worldview that considers individuals as socially embedded individual within the social structures and not as atomistic individual who has limited insights of behavior in social interactions is significant to give a complete picture of how human nature should be.

In trying to find alternative to the *homo economicus*, some economists have offered other kind of actor who is having more integrated and comprehensive behavior as alternative. They reject the idea that economic man's character that is represented by *homo economicus* as a valid stage of human development since homo economicus focused only on material growths. A broader conception of man along with our economic inquiries that focused also on human development in a broader scope is urgent to be envisaged (Tomer, 2001: 291). Some other economic agents are offered such as *homo sociologicus* who concern with the group interests; *homo socio-economicus* who is other-centered, communal, dependent, alike, and culture bound (O'Boyle, 2005: 489); *homo institutional economicus,* who is strongly influenced by institutions and learns from his social and technical experience; *homo humanistic economicus,* who has a strong tendency to develop and continually moving from the lower self (reflecting the material needs) toward higher self or toward self-actualization (Tomer, 2001: 287-288). Zafirovski (2003) suggests *homo complexicus* that incorporates and tries to integrate all these "hominess'.

Islamic economics, however, offers *homo Islamicus.* A man who is equipped himself with Islamic values in all his behaviors. The concept is created based on Islamic worldview which is a comprehensive worldview that does not dichotomize the divine and mundane, the moral and ethics, body and soul, *dunya* (the world) and *akhirah* (hereafter) in its view on the nature of man. Islamic economics considers man to have all these characteristics in his behavior. His self and characteristics is not inclined to one particular side that make him self as a "half-person" and will make his behavior imbalance or incline to only one side as in conventional economics.

The notion of Islamic man (*homo Islamicus*) is derived from Islamic methodology which considers sources of knowledge are not limited to intellectual reasoning and fact observation. Revealed knowledge (*wahy*) in Islamic economics is considered as a primary source of knowledge. Islamic economics derives the notion of *homo Islamicus* from revealed knowledge (Qur'an and Sunnah) together with intellectual reasoning and some fact observations of nature of man. Therefore, the concept of man behavior in Islamic economics is somewhat different from conventional economics that utilize "methodological individualism" in conceiving economic man behavior.

Finally, both economic agent compared in this paper is constructed from certain worldview. Homo economicus is a creature of the capitalist system and reflects the essence of this system. He is an ideological construction that comes in package with a whole set of values that imposed on him, although the proponents of positive economics who have put those values repeatedly claimed it as a value-free concept and fully reflect the fact as it is. *Homo Islamicus* on the other hand, is also an ideological construction of the Islamic economic system. He is created based on the ideals of the nature of human being behavior that is envisaged in Islamic teachings (Qur'an and Sunnah). Both, *homo economicus* and *homo Islamicus* are conscious of ther worldview/ideology in their actual economic behavior. His development and progress is structured based on this ideological consciousness. The more he is closer to the 'ideals', the more he achieves progress.

REFERENCES

Abelson, Raziel and Nielsen, Kai (2006). The History of Ethics. In *Encyclopedia of Philosophy*, 2nd Edition (ed. Donald M. Borchert). USA: Thomson Gale (394-439).

Ahmad, Khursyid. (1992). Nature and significance of Islamic Economics. In Ausaf Ahmad and Kazim Raza Awan (eds.), *Lectures on Islamic economics* (pp. 19-31). Jeddah: IRTI – IDB.

Al-Attās, Syed Muhammad Naquib. (1993). *Islām and secularism.* Kuala Lumpur: ISTAC.

Al-Faruqi, Ismail Raji. (1992). *Al-Tawhid: Its Implication for Thought and Life.* Herndon, USA: IIIT.

Arif, Muhammad. (1985). Towards a Definition of Islamic Economics: Some Scientific Consideration. *Journal of Research in Islamic Economics,* 2 (2): 87-103.

Baghirathan et al. (2004). Structuralist economics: worldly philosophers, models, and methodology. *Social Research,* summer.

Bakar, Osman. (1997). *Islam and Civilizational Dialogue: The Quest for A Truly Universal Civilization.* Kuala Lumpur, University Malaya Press

Choudhury, Masudul Alam. (1986). *Contributions to Islamic economic theory: A study in social economics.* New York: St. Martin's Press.

Davis, John B. (2003). *The theory of the individual in economics: identity and value.* London: Routledge.

Furqani, Hafas. (2006). *Ontology and Methodology of Contemporary Islamic Economics: A Preliminary Exploration.* Unpublished Master thesis. International Islamic University Malaysia.

Friedman, Milton. (1953). *Essays in positive economics.* Chicago: Univ. of Chicago Press.

Golshani, Mehdi. (2000). How to Make Sense of 'Islamic Science'?. *AJISS 17* (3), 1-21.

Heilbroner, Robert. (1988). *Behind the veil of economics.* Ontario: W.W. Norton and Company.

Heilbroner, Robert. (1999).*The worldly philosophers* (7th edn.). New York: Simon and Schuster.

Hodgson, G.M. (1988). *Economics and Institutions.* Philadelphia: University of Pennsylvania Press.

Izutsu, Toshihiko. (2002, [1964]). *God and Man in the Qur'an: Semantics of the Qur'anic Weltanschauung.* Kuala Lumpur: Islamic Book Trust.

Kahf, Monzer. (2003). Islamic economics: Notes on definition and methodology. *Review of Islamic Economics, 13,* 23-47.

Khaliq, Abdul. (1992). Faith and Morality: The Islamic View. *AJISS, 9*(3), 305-309.

Kirzner, Israel M. (1976). *The economic point of view.* Kansas City: Sheed and Ward Inc.

Naqvi, Syed Nawab Haider. (1994). *Islam, economics and society.* London: Kegan Paul International.

Nasr, Syeed Hossein. (1981). *Islamic Life and Thought.* London: George Allen & Unwin.

Nasr, Seyyed Vali Reza. (1986). Whither Islamic economics? *Islamic Quarterly, 30* (4), 211-220.

Mannan, M. A. (1984). *The Making of Islamic Economic Society.* Jeddah, Saudi Arabia: Islamic Research and Training Institute, King Abdul Aziz University.

Myers, Milton L. (1983). *The Soul of Modern Economic Man: Ideas of self-Interest, Thomas Hobbes to Adam Smith.* Chicago: University of Chicago Press.

O'Boyle, Edward J. (2005). Homo Socio-Economicus: Foundational to Social Economics and the Social Economy. *Review of Social Economy, LXIII* (3), 483-507.

Poolack, Detlef. (2008). Introduction: Religious Change in Modern Societies – Perspectives Offered by the Sociology of Religion. In Detlef Pollack and Daniel V.A. Olson (eds.), *The Role of Religion in Modern Societies,* (pp. 1-22). New York: Routledge.

Qutb, Sayyid. (1991). *The Islamic Concept and Its Characteristics (Khasais al-Tassawwur al-Islami wa Muqawwamatihi).* Translated by Mohammed Moinuddin Siddiqui. Plainfield, USA: American Trust Publication.

Ryan, Frank X. (2003). Values as consequences of transaction: commentary on 'Reconciling *homo economicus* and John Dewey's ethics'. *Journal of Economic Methodology 10* (2), 245–257.

Samuelson, Paul A. (1952). Economic Theory and Mathematics: An Appraisal. *American Economic Review, 42,* 56-69.

Schumpeter, J.A. (1954). *History of economic analysis.* London: George Allen and Unwin.

Sen, A. (1990). *On Ethics and Economics.* Oxford: Basil Blackwell.

Sexton, Robert L. (2006). *Essential of Economics.*2nd edition. USA: Thomson Higher Education.

Spengler, Joseph J. (1980). *Origins of economic thought and justice.* USA: Southern Illinois University Press.

Swidler, Leonard. (2002). Toward a universal declaration of global ethics. *Islamic Millenium Journal, 2* (2), 11-36.

Tomer, John F. (2001). Economic man vs. heterodox men: the concepts of human nature in schools of economic thought. *Journal of Socio-Economics, 30,* 281-293.

Wolozin, Harold. (2002). The individual in economic analysis: toward psychology of economic behavior. *Journal of Socio-Economics, 31,* 45–57.

Zafirovski, Milan. (2003). Human Rational Behavior and Economic Rationality. *Electronic Journal of Sociology.*

AN ISLAMIC PERSPECTIVE ON CONSUMPTION, SAVING AND INVESTMENT: TO FLOURISH A BARAKAH WEALTH OF UMMAH

Dayangku Aslinah Abd. Rahim

IntroductionIslam is the right way of religion.[29] It is a religion of *Al-Falah*[30], victory and prosperity. However in these days, Muslims, from east to west, seem to be shadowed by the problem of poverty and impoverishment. Poverty is the condition of lacking full economic access to the basic human needs such as foods, clothes, shelters, education and medicine. It is the inability to afford an adequate standard of consumption (Oxford Dictionary of Economics, 2002). Unfulfilled basic needs will lead to hunger and lack of nutrition, sickness and other ailments, homeless, freezing

---

[29] 'Then We put thee on the (right) Way of Religion: so follow thou that (Way), and follow not the desires of those who know not.' (45: 18)

[30] *Falah* refers more to success in the hereafter (Hasanuzzaman, 1997) or refers to salvation in the hereafter (Akhtar, 2000). Others defined it as material and spiritual success to gain the pleasure of Allah (Abdul Kader, 2001). *Falah* comes from the Arabic word which literally means 'success' or 'well-being.'

to death and illiteracy. From macro perspective, being destitute will steer to social crisis, retarded in spirits and disgraceful society, reduction in economic growth, less country's productivity, lack of skilled and healthy human capital and other related mess.

In Islam, poverty must not be a voluntary conduct. Islam disdains poverty in any form, chiefly because man has been created on this earth as a viceroy of Allah, and he does not like His viceroy or His progenies should pass poor life (Kalam, 1991). As mentioned by Nik Hassan (1990), poverty is not only an economic disease but also affects individual spirituality. From the viewpoint of Islam, and other religions as well, the issue of the spiritual poverty of the believers in today's world is no less important than the problem of material deprivations, which afflict the vast majority (Hassan, 1997). According to Hassan, the *Shari'ah* sees an intimate relationship between them. There was one tradition which said: "Sometimes poverty turns into disbelief," (al-Sayuti Jami-al-Saghar). The Prophet (*s.a.w*) is reported to have sought God's protection from poverty (narrated by Abu Dawud).

Early economist J.S. Mills sometimes defined economics as a study of wealth (Rosly, 2007). Every man is rich or poor according to the degree in which he can afford to enjoy the necessaries, conveniencies (conveniences), and amusements of human life (by Cantillon, as translated by Adam Smith in 'The Wealth of Nations'[31]). Islam encourages its followers to acquire wealth. Allah (SWT) clearly said in the Qur'an to disperse in the world and search for His bounty[32], and Umar (r.a), one of the *Sahabah*[33] once said: 'None of you should sit (idle) away from seeking *rizq* (livelihood), saying "Oh Allah, give me rizq," since you know that the sky does not rain gold and silver.' Some of the early Muslim scholars such as Al-Muhasibi, Al-Ghazali, Ibn Tufayl and Ibn

---

[31] Pp. 43, revised edition, 2003

[32] The Qur'an; 62:10

[33] The Beloved Prophet's companions during his lifetime.

Taimiyah also encouraged the Muslim followers to get *halal*[34] earnings by their own effort. They despised poverty and it is the society's and the state's obligation to eradicate (or reduce) the phenomenon.

Every Muslim should participate actively in economic activities. Islam does not encourage solving the problem (poverty) through short-term measures like transfer of money or value in kind (Nik Hassan, 1990). Instead, it stresses the importance for individuals to become self-reliant through participation in economic opportunities. The Qur'an says[35] that all men are created equal, but some are endowed with more talent, energy, ambition and wealth, so there are bound to be differences in degrees of economic success (Abbasi et.al., 1989). Thus, Abbasi added, that the Islamic religion accepts maldistribution of wealth and income and justifies it in the interests of efficiency; with the caveat that the wealthier people in society should be aware of their obligations to the poorer people. Poverty cannot be fully eradicated in society, but it should not be a conduct of choice. One should not choose to be poor and subjected to other people's compassion. When Allah (SWT) asked the servants to give charity[36], the Muslims should look at it in terms of the supply side, not the opposite.

Poverty can stamp a dent image on Muslims' pride, particularly if the condition is a matter of choice. The circumstance might be different if there is a lack of opportunities or a physical constraint. Some might argue that Muslims should live in moderation. The concept of moderation should no longer be used as a plea to rely on individual fate and poor living conditions (Mannan, 1984). Moreover, if the hardship is accompanied by being a burden on society, for instance, involvement in social crises, then, this is

---

[34] 'Permissible in Islam'.

[35] The Qur'an; 4:32.

[36] The Qur'an; 2:215, 2: 261-274 and 3:38-39. Sometimes the term 'charity' in the Qur'an denotes '*zakat*' (religious tax) and '*infaq*' (spending).

an offense to Islam. Muslims should always be part of society's solutions, not the opposite. They must spread their helping hands, as part of the population cannot avoid being deprived. Islam is a *'din'*, which is a representation of a whole way of life.[37] The way a Muslim presents himself, should be in accordance to Islamic fundamentals.

In today's world, the alternative to fulfilling one's needs is by making an effort to accomplish them. Consequently, Muslims should have both physical and spiritual strength in order to search for the bounties of God. Islam motivates followers to make good earnings and spend them in accordance to God's will.[38] Allah said *'earn and spend'*; hence that is what its purpose is.[39] When people have this outlook and awareness of ultimate goals, seeing wealth in "worldly" economic relation as a means, they can arrange their lives in order to reach higher aims (Taleghani, 1982). Thus, Islam should not be long associated with poverty and the typical behavior of lazy man in economic enterprises. Islam should always be synonymous with prosperity (Nik Mohamed Affandi, 2001). Haron Din (2007) has also highlighted in his book that Muslims must become rich and wealthy.

According to Rosly (2007), it is worthy to note that it is not wealth that becomes unacceptable in al-Ghazali's theory of ethics. To al-Ghazali, the famous eleventh century Islamic philosopher, it is the love of wealth and acquisition for its own sake (hubb al-mal) that he disagrees with. Islam sees wealth as a bounty from God (Kahf, 1992). According to Nik Mohamed Affandi (2001), it should be emphasized that all Muslims should acquire wealth subject to three major conditions; wealth must be accumulated in

---

[37] See Mawdudi (1991) and Haneef (1997).

[38] The Qur'an; 2:215, 219, 254, 3:134

[39] Extra reading, see Khalid Zaheer on "Islamic Economics: An Emphasis on Spending and Utilisation of Resources". (http://islamicissues.jeeran. com/kzaheer.html)

an absolutely honest manner, wealth must be managed in a highly responsible manner to benefit all and (accumulation of) wealth does not in any way distract Muslims from their strong faith in Allah (SWT). Allah (SWT) encourages Muslims to earn and disburse wealth. In economics' theories, there are several major components that contribute toward the growth of the economy; namely consumption, saving and investment. Subsequently, in this paper, there will be a review on how these three components can play their major roles in Islamic economics, and how the three could revive the economy and develop *barakah* wealth for the Muslim *ummah* and to the country in general.

Limitations of the Study

This is a qualitative and conceptual paper. Most of the traditional and contemporary writings in Islamic economics, whether extracted from research papers, articles, books, online resources, and conference papers or unpublished papers, are used and analyzed. This paper lacks of quantitative approach in its findings since the paper is based on secondary data and the writer's readings and observation. This paper discusses the components of consumption (or spending), saving and investment in moving the economy. However in macroeconomics, there are also other major components that play huge parts towards the country's economic growth such as Gross Domestic Products (GDP), inflation, government spending and international trade. Nonetheless, these terms are not discussed and analyzed in this paper.

Wealth and Consumption from Islamic perspective

Islam creates a harmony between the material and the moral by urging Muslims to strive for material welfare but stressing simultaneously that they place this material effort on a moral foundation (Chapra, 2005). According to Chapra, in this pursuit of a prosperous life, it is possible for a Muslim to go to the extreme and to make material welfare an end in itself by ignoring spiritual values, acquiring wealth through unfair means, exploiting others, subjecting to wrong and injustice, and by not promoting the good of others from what he has earned or accumulated. Hence, Islam also seeks to purify life, as Allah (SWT) clearly warns Muslims against this danger: 'When the prayer is ended then disperse in the land and seek of God's bounty but remember God much so that you may be successful' (62:10).

Every Muslim should as such earnestly struggle to acquire at least some wealth (Nik Mohamed Affandi, 2001). Wealth is supposed to be acquired and disposed in accordance with *shariah*. Al-Ghazali has placed knowledge (*'ilm*), wealth, influence, family and noble birth (i.e. in a religious family) as some of the external goods (*al-fada'il al-kharijiyya*) leading to ultimate happiness (*sa'adat haqiqiya*) (Rosly, 2007). However, the purpose of economic strength is not to accumulate wealth. Allah said: 'Who pileth up wealth and layeth it by, Thinking that his wealth would make him last forever!'[40] Wealth is not supposed to be left idle. Idle money exposes to devaluation through inflation. Idle wealth is also subjected to *zakat*, and relatively, unproductive and unused wealth has a tendency to have higher rates. Higher rate of zakat is good if the assets itself is productive. *Zakat* is an effective instrument to eliminate wasteful and unproductive assets in Islamic society (Afzal-Ur-Rahman, 1991).

In order to gain income or to combat poverty, there are six solutions suggested by Yusof Al-Qardawi (translated, 2005). The first and foremost is by working or own effort. Every Muslim must struggle to meet an end, either by getting a paid job or by making one. The second solution is by receiving aid from his/ her own well-off family. Relationship within families has strong bond in nature. Thus, children, parents, siblings and relatives are the closest relations and have direct contact between each other.

---

[40] The Qur'an; 104: 2-4

The Qur'an says: 'But kindred by blood have prior rights against each other in the Book of God.' (8:75). The other four suggestions to alleviate poverty are from *zakat,* government fund, society's concern and charity help. From this proposal, the responsibility of acquiring wealth lies in individual's hand, and then through government and society.

Earning an honest income is essential in Islam (Nik Mohamed Affandi, 2002). Yet again, income and wealth is meant to be spent. Spending here refers to paying out the earnings. Spending, which the root word is 'spend' means to use up or pay out (money) (The New penguin English Dictionary, 2000). In economics, spending[41] is more known as (and always be referred to as) consumption, which means spending for survival or enjoyment, as opposed to providing future production (Oxford Dictionary of Economics, 2002). According to Mankiw (2007), consumption means spending by households on goods and services, with the exception of purchases of new housing (which economists categorize buying a new housing as investment). According to Kahf (1992), the act of use or consumptions of good things is in itself considered as a virtue in Islam, since the enjoyment of what Allah creates for mankind is obedience to Him.

Consumption in Islam is subjected to the Law of God. In other words, there will be some obligations and ethics to follow. In general, there are 3 stages of human needs, namely; 1) Necessities or basic needs[42] such as food, clothes, shelters, education, medicines and security, 2) Necessaries where some things that can make life more comfortable or enhance basic needs such as better food, bigger house and more clothing and 3) Luxury

---

[41] The term spending and consumption will be used interchangeably throughout this paper.

[42] Chapra, 1985, has enunciated six basic needs, which include: education and training, employment, adequate food and clothing, comfortable housing, medical facilities and an adequate transport facilities.

(or semi-luxury). For the first requirement, every man (and his family) must be permitted to the basic needs, either by own effort or if necessary, with the help from the authorities and NGO's.[43] As to al-Ghazali, an individual who possesses ample wealth should be able to devote more time to knowledge (*'ilm*) and action (*amal*), for he is free from the care of the necessities of life (Rosly, 2007). Thus, each Muslim man must spend for the basic provisions of himself and his family.

In terms of spending for necessaries, some Muslims might feel there is no objection to live more comfortably. However, there is an issue regarding spending for luxury. The Prophet (s.a.w) also said that Allah detests those who are being reckless in spending[44]. Waste things and unnecessary hoarding is not permitted in Islam. According to Nik Mohamed Affandi (2001), Islam condemns wasteful consumption. He added that wasteful spending is disallowed even for consumption of basic necessities such as food and clothing. Overly consumption of luxurious goods is regarded as extravagance and gross wastefulness. To Akram Khan (1994), the Islamic view of life would require that those who can afford to have a higher material standard should voluntarily forego some of their comforts and help others (to) improve their

---

[43] Muhammad Yunus, the founder of the Grameen Bank and the winner of the Nobel Peace Prize, once asked (before the existence of the Grameen Bank), what would he do if he is the President of the World Bank? Interestingly, he answered: to move the headquarters to Dhaka; The overarching objective of the World Bank is to combat world poverty, then it seems the bank should be moved to a location where poverty is at its worst. In Dhaka, the World Bank would be surrounded by human suffering and destitution. By living in close proximity to the problem, bank officials might be able to solve it faster and more realistically.

[44] Shahih Bukhary, pp. 270.

economic lot so as to enjoy a similar life-style.[45] Even, if the result is not really a similar life-style, but at least the gap between the poor and the rich could be reduced. Development and progress are rather meaningless to a Muslim community if there exists a wide income gap between rich and poor (Nik Mohamed Affandi, 2001).

To continue, besides over consumption, Allah also forbids spending in a wrong way or *haram* production. According to Kahf, Muslims should avoid an act of extravagance (*israf*) or profligacy (*tabthir*). Profligacy means spending in the wrong way, e.g. on prohibited activities such as bribery, on illegal things, or in a reckless manner. Extravagance means overspending on lawful matters such as food, clothes, shelter, or even charity. He added that the Islamic teachings recommend a moderate and balance pattern of consumption and spending, a pattern which lies in between miserliness and extravagance. Consumption above and beyond the moderate level is considered *israf* and is condemned. Consumption and satisfaction (utility) are not condemned in Islam as long as they do not involve any harm or harmful things.

In Islam, consumption is not just limited to spend on goods and services, tangible or non-tangible. Reaching out to the poor or the needy could also be called spending in a way of Allah (swt). Allah (swt) said: 'Those who spend their wealth for increase in self-purification.'[46] Allah (swt) also said: 'O ye who believe! Give of the good things which ye have (honorably) earned,' 'And whatever ye spend in charity or devotion, be sure God knows it all.', '... They ask thee how much they are to spend; Say: "What is beyond your needs".'[47] Allah (swt) also said; '.... And there are those who bury gold and silver and spend it not in the Way of

---

[45] However, according to him, the kind of economy that seems to harmonize with the Islamic ethos is a low consumption economy, in which, the writer finds hard to agree with.

[46] The Qur'an; 92: 19

[47] The Qur'an; 2: 267, 2: 270, 2: 219

God: announce unto them a most grievous penalty.[48'] From these verses, spending (or *infaq*) refers more to the deed of charity or the obligation of paying *zakat*. Abu Hurairah (*r.a.*), reported that the Prophet (s.a.w) mentioned that those who spend for his family, women, children and the poor will be closed to them in heaven, and the deed is equal as going to the war in the path of Allah (*fi sabilillah*)[49].

In another hadith, the Prophet (s.a.w) said, to those who have enough food for two, should eat with three people (al-Jammal, translated, 2000). Islam promotes brotherhood among the *ummah* and sharing is one of the culture. In consequence, besides spending for himself and his family, a Muslim should also share the wealth with others. This can be done by paying out the obligatory *zakat*[50] and voluntary charity such as *sadaqah* and *waqf*. The contribution of *zakat* and charity should be given through the right channels, such as via Islamic government and institutions. However, direct donation is appropriate in certain situations such as to closest poor relatives and neighbours or to those in needs surround us. For those Muslims who are already wealthy, they should as earnestly attempt to eradicate poverty among Muslim communities (Nik Mohamed Affandi, 2001). Accordingly, everyone should be motivated to earn and spend in the cause of Allah. Islam is a religion of right people who spand in charity and way of Allah (swt).

The world is a trial to mankind as it is packed with lots of enchanting things[51] where sometimes man forgets himself. Allah (swt) summons him to earn wealth but he forgets to spend accordingly. Thus he accumulates wealth and gains the usufruct

---

[48] The Qur'an; 9: 34

[49] Shahih Muslim, translated, pp. 394-5.

[50] There are two kind of zakat (or zakah): Zakat Eid-ul-Fitri and zakat on all surplus wealth and agricultural income of the Muslims.

[51] The Qur'an; 64: 15 - 16

for himself alone without any consideration of society. Hence, God would condemn those who are hoarding it or spend wealth unwisely[52]. Therefore, it is crucial if the wealth goes to the right hands. In an Islamic society, *taqwa* (God-consciousness) is considered very highly (Akram Khan, 1994). Akram added that the more a person is God-conscious, the more highly he is esteemed in the society. Hence, only God-conscious man will put the right things onto its place. To sum up, in Islam, a man must spend his wealth according to God's will and this will earn the blessing from Allah (swt). None is the greatest gift from God, but a blessed and *barakah* life.

Saving and Investment in Islam

In modern economics' theory, whichever earnings that man does not spend, is called saving. Saving is the excess of income over consumption (Oxford Dictionary of Economics, 2002). Saving is the part of income which is not consumed; in other words, the difference between disposable income (take-home pay) and consumption (Samuelson & Nordhaus, 1995). As for investment, it could be defined from two approaches. According to Samuelson *et. al*, it is an economic activity that forgoes consumption today with an eye to increasing output in the future. It includes tangible capitals such as equipments and intangible investments such as education. In finance terms, investment denotes the purchase of security, such as a stock or a bond. To Oxford Dictionary of Economics (2002), investment is the process of adding to stocks of real productive assets, which may mean acquiring fixed assets such as buildings. On the other hand, investment also means the acquisition of financial assets such as company shares.

To simplify, in general, if a man does not spend all of his income, he can save his unused income. For this paper, saving and investment will be looked up from both finance and economic

---

[52] The Qur'an; 17: 26 - 27

perspectives. In economy (closed economy) as a whole, whatever is available by saving, will be available for investment (S = I). In practice, most people do save, at least for everyday expenses or for some emergency needs. Some put aside some unused money to increase standard of living or for retirement purposes, while others accumulate wealth for bequest and legacy to the families and their future generations. Yet, there also some cases exist where they invest their money for the purpose of accumulating wealth; where they enjoy seeing the money assets increase day after day. It is a kind of self-satisfaction so that they can enjoy spending money without any worry or limit.

Islamic economic system has opposed any form of investment in non-productive activities particularly in a kind of activity that accumulates wealth as much as possible (Ataul Huq, translated, 1998). According to Ataul Huq, among the economic effects of paying *zakat* are the incentives to invest and to save. Wealth and money should be circulated and do not just be concentrated only in a few hands[53]. This could lead to a monopoly of some wealthy people and an increase of gap between poor and rich. Accordingly, the obligation of paying *zakat* and the involvement in another charity would purify the fortunes and the payer themselves. The motivation to pay *zakat* (and other aid as well) will lead to the incentive to save. Allah (swt) does not like hoarded wealth. Islam encourages a mobilization of saving to produce a balanced economic development (Sarimah Hanim, 2006). According to Sarimah, Islam promotes development of productive saving, for instance through good investment. Thus the incentive to save will lead to investment.

Islam promotes saving and investment. Money should be saved through productive ways. This means that saving should be put into financial intermediaries that help to mobilize the assets, if the owner does not want or do not have any expertise/

---

[53] The Qur'an; 59: 8

time to stimulate the additional money himself. However, any involvement in interest-based activities is forbidden. Many scholars are unanimous that interest is similar to riba and riba is haram in Islam[54]. Nowadays, there is an alternative to the existing conventional finance and banking. Islamic banking and finance could be utilized to cater Muslim's need in mobilizing funds. Unlike the interest-based system that is a zero-sum game, Islam promotes or encourages a positive-sum game where all parties gain, or at least there is a possibility of gain and loss of both parties (Bakar, 2008). According to Bakar, this may take the form of both equity and debt financing that assumes a certain degree of risk and liability to justify the lawfulness of income or yield earned from those transactions.

To re-emphasize, besides banks, other financial intermediaries and markets that are available such as Islamic insurance or *takaful*, unit trust, capital market and money market whose products and activities are screened by *shariah* experts or advisors. In another words, the activities of Islamic banking and finance should not involve prohibited business of goods and services from Islamic perspective. As the Islamic financial system is based on the *shariah*, it also means that the services rendered by the system, namely risk-sharing, liquidity and information must also be *shariah*-driven (Rosly, 2007). According to Bakar (2008), Islamic banking products are both religiously appealing and financially viable. From the management point of view, Islamic banking (and

---

[54] There are three stages of prohibition of riba from Al-Qur'an: 1) 30: 39 (and 4: 161 ~ Told us the story of Jews taking riba), 2) 3: 130 – 132 (Prevent man to take usury, doubled or multiplied) and 3) 2: 275 – 281 (Those who said trade is similar to riba; while God permits trade and forbids usury) – Rosly, 2007. Other interesting readings on riba, see 'An Introduction to Islamic Economics & Finance' (2005) published by CERT.

finance) could be considered as a mode of diversification that has been proven to be the best method to manage risk.

By saving or depositing some income in any financial institution, the saver is actually supplying capital to the deficit sector. It might look a small contribution for him but large number of savers will create high volumes of surplus. This creates win-win situation between the savers and the financial intermediaries. Savers need convenience and good protections of their asset for the future and financial institutions require funds to do the business dealings with[55]. Nonetheless, those who prone for being risk-takers would do a different kind of saving, which they are willing to share either the profit or the loss with the financial institutions. In this scenario, they are investors, from finance perspective. The risk-takers could either come from surplus sector or deficit sector. From surplus sector, for instance, they are capital provider. Nevertheless, they are capital user, if they are in deficit or demand sector.

Islam encourages Muslims to invest their money and to become partners in order to share profits and risks in the business instead of becoming creditors (Salamon, 2004). As defined in the *shariah* (Islamic Law), Islamic finance is based on the belief that the provider of capital and the user of capital should equally share the risk of business ventures, be it from industries, farms, service companies or simple trade deals (Siddiqi, 1987). According to Salamon (2004), Islam is not willing to allow a loophole to exist for those who do not wish to invest and take risks but rather are content with hoarding money or depositing money in a bank

---

[55] In this situation, the intention of saving is genuine, thus savings' principal should be guaranteed to be returned (*ceteris paribus*). Any surplus or *hibah* is optional. This kind of saving usually refers to wadiah or saving account in contemporary banks.

in return for receiving an increase on these funds[56] for no risk
(other than the bank becoming insolvent). He added that Islam
encourages the notion of higher risks and higher returns and
promotes it by leaving no other avenue available to investors as the
objective is that high-risk investments provide a stimulus to the
economy and encourage entrepreneurs to maximize their effort.

In addition, for a small amount of money, it might give no
harm to be part of actual saving or deposit. This cash usually
acts as a contingency needs or for day by day expenditure where
most people do not want to carry a sum amount of money in their
wallets. Conversely, for an extra and excess amount of unused
money, it should be injected into the economy as investment
(e.g. buying Islamic shares and *sukuk* (Islamic-biased equities
and bonds), joining mudarabah or musyarakah, etc). The more
money is being disseminated in the economy, the more it can buy
goods and services. This can appreciate the value of the country's
currency and make every cent more worthy. When it comes to
deciding where to place one's investments, the first set of filters is
quite straightforward: exclude all companies (by direct or indirect
approach) whose primary business involves forbidden products
(e.g. alcohol, pork, tobacco, (interest-based) financial services,
(destructive) weapon production, and entertainment) (Venardos,
2005).[57]

Some Recommendations

In Islam, consumption, saving and investment could revitalize
and flourish a *barakah* wealth of the Muslim *ummah*. Here are
some recommendations on how a Muslim should promote these

---

[56] It is the practice of Islamic banks today to give *hibah* (surplus) to
depositors.

[57] A typical screen given by the Dow Jones Islamic Index (DJII) Shariah
board (www.dowjones.com/corp/index_products.htm)

habits so that he could be one of the contributors to the economic growth and development:

A. Consumption

1. A Muslim should acquire some wealth so that he could be able to devote more time to good deeds and action (*amal*), for he is free from the care of some basic necessities.
2. A Muslim should spend for the basic provisions of himself and his family.
3. Begging or pleading is not the culture of Islam.
4. Muslims are required to allocate some of his earnings to benefit his children in the future.[58]
5. A Muslim should acquire some wealth so that he would be able to assist other fellows, starting from the near families and relatives.
6. A Muslim must spend for the obligatory zakat and voluntary charity.
7. A Muslim ought to avoid wasteful spending and wrong way of consumption.
8. A Muslim should keep away from spending on prohibited goods and services.

B. Saving and Investment

1. It is essential for a Muslim to save some of his income in most productive ways.
2. Savings, in terms of small deposit, might be suitable for daily expenses or for unforeseen events.

---

[58] Rasulullah s.a.w had told the *sahabah* to provide some wealth to their children so that the family will not be pleading or begging in the future.

3. Wealth could not be left idle, thus one alternative in how to do with the money surplus (besides spending for provisions or charity) is by carrying out investment.
4. Investment must be channeled from and through halal activities in Islam.
5. Islamic banking and financial institutions provide various ways in how to manage wealth.
6. A Muslim could also be an investor and entrepreneur himself[59]; by doing good business and administer the wealth accordingly.
7. The Islamic economy allows private enterprise by individuals and does not bind them in any other way except that business should be conducted within the bonds of the *shariah*.[60]
8. Worldly goods could deviate a man from God[61], yet a God-conscious man will bring wealth as a medium to be close to Allah.
9. A rich Muslim, who is God-conscious and pious will put the worldly wealth into the right place (avoiding *zulm*).
10. Good conduct of managing fortune will flourish a *barakah* wealth.
11. Government intervention is essential for any misconduct in production, consumption, allocation and distribution of resources and wealth.

---

[59] Rasulullah said: Nine out of ten *rizq* is in tijarah (business), by al-Sajazi. (Al-Jammal, 2000)
[60] Akram Khan, 2005 in 'An Introduction to Islamic Economics & Finance', chapter 11.
[61] See Shahih Muslim, 1997, pp. 387-8. A story of Rasulullah s.a.w by Amru Bin Auf r.a.

Conclusion

To conclude, a Muslim should obtain some wealth and be able to provide for himself and his family. He must also be rich if he wants to pay zakat and perform charity. In addition, he must do some saving in order to endow bequest to his family. Saving must not be immobile, thus he is encouraged to invest his money in appropriate ways. He, who does this, will become the 'upper' hand[62] in the society. Aggregately, a large number of this man will make the society to be economically strong and socially esteemed.

In consequence, it is a hope that this paper will support the initiative to wake up every Muslim from any lack of spirit to acquire wealth. The study could also be a stepping-stone to urge the Muslim followers to arise from their feelings of laziness, dependence and misleading moderation. Moderation in life should not be looked upon as to dampen the motivation for economic pursuits. In brief, Islam motivates its followers to pursue economic enterprises. Consumption, saving and investment could revive the economy of the ummah. *Barakah* wealth will lead its owner and his family to a blessed life. This could be one way to achieve *al-falah* provided that the behaviour and conducts should be in accordance with the prescribed rules and regulations in Islam, insya Allah.

---

[62] In Islam, giving hands are better than receiving hands. A generous hand is at top of receiving hand. From Anas r.a, Rasulullah s.a.w. said that one sign of a mu'min (devout Muslim) is to love the ansar. Ansar, during that period of time, are group of Madinah people who helped the Muhajirin, a group that moved to Madinah from Makah.

REFERENCES

Abul Kalam, S.M. 1991. The Basic Principles of Islamic Economics. *Journal of Islamic Banking and Finance.* 8 (3).

Adam Smith. 1776. The Wealth of Nations (5th Edition - 2003). Bantam Classic.

Afzal-Ur-Rahman. 1991. Doktrin Ekonomi Islam Jilid III. (Penterjemah: Zaharah Salleh). Kuala Lumpur: Dewan Bahasa dan Pustaka

Akram Khan, M. 1994. *An Introduction to Islamic Economics.* International Institute of Islamic Thought and Institute of Policy Studies. Islamabad.

Akram Khan, Muhammad. 2005. Types of Business Organisation in an Islamic Economy. In a book entitled 'An Introduction to Islamic Economics & Finance' Edited by Sheikh Ghazali Sheikh Abod et. al. Kuala Lumpur: CERT Publications.

Al-Jammal, Muhammad Abdul Mun'im, 2000. ensiklopedia Ekonomi Islam Jilid 1 (Penterjemah: Salahuddin Abdullah). Kuala Lumpur: Dewan Bahasa dan Pustaka.

Bakar, Mohd. Daud. 2008. Riba and Islamic Banking and Finance. In a book entitled 'Essesntial Readings in Islamic Finance' Edited by Mohd. Daud Bakar and Engku Rabiah Adawiah. Kuala Lumpur: CERT Publications.

Chapra, M. Umar. 1985. The Islamic Welfare State and its Role in the Economy. U.K: The Islamic Foundation.

Chapra, Muhammad Umar. 2005. Objectives of the Islamic Economics Order. In a book entitled 'An Introduction to Islamic Economics & Finance' Edited by Sheikh Ghazali Sheikh Abod et. al. Kuala Lumpur: CERT Publications.

Haneef, Mohamed Aslam. 1997. Islam, the Islamic Worldview and Islamic Economics. *IIUM Journal of Economics and Management*. 5 (1).

Haron Din. 2007. Islam: Agama, Bisnes dan Pengurusan. Kuala Lumpur. PTS Publications & Distributions.

Hassan, Zubair. 1997. Fulfillment of Basic needs: Concept, Measurement, and Muslim Countries' Performance. *IIUM Journal of Islamic economics and Management* 5. 2.

Kahf, Monzer. 1992. The Theory of Consumption. In a book entitled 'Readings in Microeconomics: An Islamic Perspective' Edited by Sayyid Tahir. al. Selangor: Longman Malaysia.

Mankiw, N.Gregory, 2007. Principles of Macroeconomics. (4th Edition). USA: Thomson South-Western.

Mannan, Abdul. 1986. *Islamic Economics: Theory and Practice*. The Islamic Academy Cambridge.

Mawdudi, Sayyid Abul A'la. 1991. *Let Us Be Muslims*. Kuala Lumpur: The Islamic Foundation, A.S. Noordeen.

Nik Hassan, Nik Mustapha. 1990. Islamisation of Malaysian Economy: A Philosophical Approach. *Lights on Islamic Economics*. 2 (1).

Nik Mohamed Affandi Nik Yusoff. 2001. Islam & Wealth: The Banlanced Approach to Wealth Creation, Accumulation and Distribtuion. Selangor: Pelanduk

Nik Mohamed Affandi Nik Yusoff. 2002. Islam & Business. Selangor: Pelanduk

Oxford Dictionary of Economics. 2003. Oxford University Press.

Pramanik, Ataul Huq, 1998. Pembangunan & Pengagihan dalam Islam (Penterjermah: Amar Said). Kuala Lumpur: Dewan Bahasa dan Pustaka.

Rosly, Saiful Azhar. 2005. Critical Issues on Islamic Banking and Financial Markets. Kuala Lumpur: Dinamas Publishing.

Salamon, Husin. 2004. The Islamic Banking System in Malaysia: Concept, Operation, Challenges and Prospects. In a book entitled 'Islamic Banking: An International Perspective' Edited by Bala Shanmugam et. al. Serdang: Universiti Putra Malaysia Press.

Sami M. Abbasi, Kenneth W. Hollman and Joe H. Murrey. 1989. Islamic Economics: Foundations and Practices. *International Journal of Social Economics.* 16 (5).

Samuelson, Paul A. & Nordhaus, William D. 1995. Economics (15ᵗʰ edition). McGraw-Hill, inc.

Sarimah Hanim Aman Shah. 2006. Ekonomi dari perspektif Islam. Selangor: Penerbit Fajar Bakti Sdn. Bhd.

Shahih Bukhary. 2000. (Malay edition). Jilid I, II & III, Kuala Lumpur: Victory Agencie.

Shahih Bukhary. 2000. (Malay edition). Jilid IV, V & VI, Kuala Lumpur: Victory Agencie.

Shahih Muslim. 1997. (Terjermahan Hadis). Jilid I, II, III & IV. Selangor: Klang Book Centre.

Taleghani, Ayatullah Sayyid Mahmud. 1982. *Features of Islamic Economics.* Society and Economics in Islam. US: Mizan Press. Berkeley.

The New Penguin English Dictionary, 2000. England: Penguin Books.

Venardos, Angelo M. 2005. Islamic Banking & Finance in South-East Asia: Its Development & Future. USA: World Scientific.

Yusof 'Ali, Abdullah. 2001. *The Holy Qur'an.* Saba Islamic Media.

Yusuf Al-Qaradawi. 2005. (Cetakan kedua – Terjemahan). Kemiskinan dan Cara islam Mengatasinya. (Penterjemah: Arsil Ibrahim). Kuala Lumpur: YAPEIM.

THE DEVELOPMENT OF WAQF INSTITUTION IN MALAYSIA: A STUDY FROM HISTORICAL AND CONTEMPORARY PERSPECTIVES

A Rahman Tang Abdullah

Introduction

This paper discusses the origin and the developmental aspects of Waqf as a religious institution in Malaysia from historical and contemporary perspectives. It is preceded by examining waqf as formal religious institution in the states in Malaysia, its process of legislation and its relations with the Islamic Charitable institutions. It also examines waqf as a dynamic institution through commercial and charitable means. One of the means to achieve this is the concept and practice of istibdal as dynamic instrument rather than a diversion from the spirit of Waqf institution.

Waqf and Charity

Waqf is always related to charity. Charity is referred to any kind of contribution which promotes welfare to the society. As a whole, the most identical form of charity is related to wealth such as property, equipments and money. It also includes other form of non-money contribution such as physical energy and voluntary services. In principle, all kind of these contributions are not motivated by any kind of material return or based on profit making.[63]

In Islam, Charity and welfare are referred to zakat (obligatory religious payment), sadaqah (religious donation) and waqf (religious charitable foundation). In this respect, waqf is applied to property and money while zakat and sadaqah are exclusively in the forms of money and food. In many respects, it has to be confessed that wealth is always considered as the primary element for the creation of welfare activities and institutions in the society. It means that certain proportion of wealth belonging to individuals, business enterprises and governmental institutions has to be disposed for financing those welfare activities and institutions.

The Concept of Philanthropy in Islam

Of course, Islam calls every capable person to goodness, whether he is rich or poor. If he is rich then he can do good with his wealth and his position of influence, and if he is poor, he can do good with his hand, his heart, his tongue and his deed. Under the Islamic order, there can be no person who cannot do good in one way or another.

Thus, in context of the existence of waqf and other religious endowment, it is concerned with the establishment of institutions based on welfare and social solidarity which are associated with philanthropy. In the case of waqf, it is really associated with the philanthropic concept of the Muslim *Ummah in which the rich had the motivation in doing good and pious work in order to seek pleasure of Allah. Here, it is reflected by the* role of the rich to donate their wealth to the Muslims especially the poor, orphans,

---

[63] Raymond W. Y. Kao, *Entrepreneurism : a philosophy and a sensible alternative for the market economy*, London: (2001), Imperial College Press, Pp. 412-26.

old men and so on. This practice is highly appreciated by Allah the Mighty as it is expressed in the Qur'an as follows:

"By no means shall you attain righteousness unless you give freely of that which you love and whatever you give, of a truth God knoweth it well". (Surah Ali Imran: 92)

The first institution of Waqf was established by Umar Ibn Al-Khattab during the time of the Prophet (peace be upon Him) in the seventh year of Hijrah. In that year, after the battle of Khaybar, Umar had acquired a parcel of land as *Ghanimah* and he had sought the advice of the Prophet regarding its use. The Prophet replied : "if you wish, retain the real and devote the usufruct to pious purpose." Umar then dedicated the land on condition that the land should not be sold or made the subject of a gift or inheritance. Later on, many Muslims emulated Umar's move. The most distinguished example can be found when Salahuddin al-Ayyubi spent all his wealth in public welfare -works and donated the lands of Syria and Egypt to welfare institutions such as mosques, schools, lodgings for travellers and other such institutions.[64]

Here, it is noteworthy to emphasize the importance of the rich without refuting the constructive role of the poor who could do good in the form of non-monetary contribution. Islam calls the rich to throw away their human instincts of greed. Poor are reminded with the satanic whispers of fear of poverty. The Qur'an encourages the believers to have faith in the way of Allah, but the Qur'an also warns that "Satan threatens you with poverty and bids you to conduct unseemly. Allah has promised you His forgiveness and bounties" (Quran, 2:268).

According to Murat Cizakca, the institution of waqf is simply defined as philanthropic foundation. This is because most of waqf

---

[64] Mustafa Siba'I, *The Islamic Civilization*, translation revised by S.M. Hasan al-Banna, Swansea, UK: (2002), Awakening Publications, p. 134-5.

properties and institutions are derived from the privately owned properties and are disposed for charitable purposes in perpetuity and in the case where the revenue is generated from those sources, it is also spent for charitable purpose. This institution of waqf stands out as one of the greatest achievements of Islamic civilization due to the fact that throughout the vast Islamic world, from the Atlantic to the Pacific, magnificent works of architecture as well as a wealth of services vitally important to the society have been financed and maintained for centuries through this system. Some of those waqfs had survived for considerably longer than half a millennium and some even for more than a millennium.[65] The longest survived waqf institution as known to the Muslims until today is the al-Azhar University in Cairo.[66]

Murat Cizakca has also successfully proved the relevance of the waqf system to economic dimension for modern Islamic societies. He argues that waqf system had provided essential services at no cost to the government such as health, education, and so on. The waqf is in fact is derived from voluntary donations. The most constructive means of donation should come from privately accumulated capital which is voluntarily endowed to finance all sorts of social services to the society. However, the success in social and economic contributions of the waqf system as a whole is based on the expectation that the waqfs are managed by prudent and efficient trust.[67]

---

[65] Murat Cizakca, *A history of philanthropic foundations: the Islamic world from the seventh century to the present*, Istanbul: (2000), Bogazici University Press p. 1.

[66] Siti Mashitah Mahamood, Wakf in Malaysia: Legal and Administrative Perspective, Kuala Lumpur: (2006), University of Malaya Press, p. 3.

[67] Murat Cizakca, Op cit., p. 2.

The origin of Waqf in Malaysia

It is a generally believed that the institution of waqf had long been established in Malaysia since Islam had become an established religion here since 15ᵗʰ century. Nevertheless, it is quite difficult to find any evidence to prove that waqf had been established during the precolonial period. Since waqf is always associated with land and property, it can be assumed that it is always created in the form of mosque, graveyard and traditional religious schools or pondok.

Nevertheless, the evidence to support this assumption is circumstantial. This is because land as the main source of waqf was not privately owned by any individual. The Malays only possess land for usage rather than private ownership.[68] Considering this fact, it can be said that the establishment of the first formal waqf institution in Malaya is Masjid Kapitan Keling in Pulau Pinang. This particular waqf is associated with its founder, Kader/Cauder Mohideen/Mydin Merican of Arab-Indian Muslim descent. He worked as a trader and travelled to Kedah Tua, Kota Kuala Muda, Acheh and other ports. He brought his family's merchandise that could bring a lot of profits, such as cotton, kayu gaharu, beads and jewels of any sorts and colours. With his hard work in trading, he became rich and earned the respect from the people of Penang and Kedah. He was also bestowed his due respects when Francis Light came to Penang. In 1801, Kader Muhiddeen Merican was officially appointed "Kapitan Keling" by the English East India Company and he was given the authority to protect, manage and administer the affairs of the Indian community. Kapitan Keling was also the right hand leader of the Chulias and they were meant

---

[68] Ahmad Nazri Abdullah, *Melayu Dan Tanah: Tumpuan Khusus Kepada Tanah Simpanan Melayu*, Media Intelek Sdn. Bhd., Kuala Lumpur, (1985), pp. 1-13.

to approach the 'kapitan' for any arising problems concerning their community or even personal life.[69]

On November 2, 1801, Lieutenant General Sir George Leith, on behalf of the English East India Company granted a piece of land (367 deeds) to the Muslim community. The west and south borders of the land met Cauder Mydin Merican's own land. After receiving a letter of authority from Governor Philips, this is where Kader Mydin Merican built the Kapitan Keling Mosque largely from his own money as well as a small contribution from the community. Kader Mydin Merican's business continued to prosper, and by 1834, he was considered as the richest Indian Muslim in Penang. His wealth, at that time, was estimated at fifty thousand Spanish dollars. As a British official, Kapitan Keling had the authority to solve any dispute involving the Muslim community that came from "Coromandel Coast", India. He passed away on 19 September 1834.[70]

It was then followed by the establishment of the second waqf institution associated with Tengku Syed Hussein Idid, the founder of Malay Mosque, Acheen Street, Penang. He was the grandson of the Sultan of Aceh and a successful and influential trader. Syed Hussein and his clan moved to Penang in 1792 and Francis Light granted him exemption from English laws. It was recognised as the first instance that the colonial administration allowed the Muslim community in the Malay Peninsula to practice the Islamic Law (Sharia) but with a condition that no capital punishment should be imposed. He set up his trading post and settlement fronting

---

[69] See Sejarah Masjid Kapitan Keling by Haji Mohamed Ismail Merican, enclosed in the conservation of Masjid Kapitan Keling, 9 January 2003, Masjid Kapitan Keling, Majlis Agama Islam Negeri Pulau Pinang (MAINPP).

[70] The Mohamedan and Hindu Endowment Board, Straits Settlements, 1926, p. 23.

the sea. The settlement was recognised as the first township in Penang and was referred to as the Malay Town or Malay enclave.

His standing as a seasoned trader with a vast trading network influenced others, especially Arabs in the Malay Archipelago, to migrate to Penang. By 1803, the Malay Town covered Acheen Street (Lebuh Aceh), Malay Street, Armenian Street and parts of Carnavon Street and Beach Street. By his will dated 1820, Syed Hussein created the wakaf for the Malay Mosque or Masjid Melayu which was constructed around 1800. The land comprises Lot 200 Town Subdivision XXII. Apart from the mosque, a total of 16 houses were erected namely houses no 103, 105, 107, 113, 115 and 117 Chulia Street and no 49, 55, 57, 59, 77, 79, 81, 81A, B and C Acheen Street.

Then, other waqf institutions were established in the form of mosque and madrasah such as Masjid Hashim Yahya, Waqf Haji Kassim, waqf majoodsaw, and Madrasah al-Masyhur in Penang. All the Waqf properties in Penang and the Straits Settlements were then legislated and governed under the Mohamedan and Hindu Endowment Board. The similar principle and practice were extended to other Malay states following the extension of British rule in Malay Peninsula in the later period. In the Malay states, all those waqf institutions were governed under Islamic Religious Enactment of the state and administered by the Islamic Religious Council of the states. This practice continued to be implemented after the independence.[71] Currently, all the waqf properties have to be legally declared and registered with the States Islamic religious Council as the trustees of the waqf properties in Malaysia. All the deeds relating to waqf are legally registered under the name of Islamic religious council of the states.

---

[71] For the Brief discussion on the establishment of Waqf institution in Malaya, see Moshe Yegar, Islam and Islamic Insttitution in British Malaya, Hebrew University Press, Jerusalem, 1979, pp. 205-16.

Commercialism and Waqf in Malaysia

In principle, when all Muslims are asked to show humility and simplicity, it actually gives the impression that Muslims should not intend to live in the impoverished and backward conditions. In fact, from economic perspective, Muslims are asked to improve their condition. The most promising means to achieve this aim is through the involvement in business activities. Currently, the most practical orientation in economic practice is market economy which is extensively based on commercialism. This is also no exception to the Muslims in Malaysia.

In many respects, the commercial orientation is closely associated with entrepreneurship or private enterprise. The only concern is to what extent in which commercialism is complemented with benevolent means in the market economy. This is to justify the objective of every private enterprise in gaining profit in their business activities by which the proportion of profit is to be disposed for humanitarian purposes. It is also necessary to consider that profit must not be gained from any course to the detriment of others.

In this context, it is very clear that the relations between entrepreneurship and charity can be found in the institution of waqf in Malaysia. This is due to the fact that the foundation of waqf properties in Malaysia is associated with the private individuals. The most distinguished example can be refered to Masjid Kapitan Keling in Pulau Pinang as it has been mentioned before.[72]

Another prominent example is Tan Seri Sayyid Mokhtar al-Bukhari from Kedah. He began his business profession as a petty businessman but eventually became a successful corporate figure. He is currently the largest share holder of DRB-HICOM. He had even allocated some portion of his revenue to help his poor

---

[72] See Open Minute on Conservation Project of Masjid Melayu at Lebuh Acheh, 11 May 1996, MAINPP.

neighbours since he was still a petty businessman. He is well known by his involvement in charitable and educational activities and founding social and cultural organizations. He established al-Bukhari Foundation and allocated funds for building mosques in a highly commercial location at Langgar in Alor Setar, Kedah and the Golden Triangle area in Kuala Lumpur. In many respects, he still preserves the long tradition of establishing identical waqf such as mosques and also provides for theirs expenditure and maintenance.[73]

Waqf and the Question of Self-reliance

It is generally accepted that the understanding of Islamic law in relation to the institution of waqf or charitable endowment means that a person has dedicated his or her property to God for the benefit of the public good for all time. However, this understanding creates many restriction on the management of waqf because it is a normal practice for the doner to specify the use of a waqf property for a specifically beneficial purpose. The charitable gift becomes public property that cannot be given away, sold, mortgaged, inherited or otherwise disposed of.

According to Muhammad Zain bin Haji Othman, the features inherent in *waqf is as follows:* Firstly, collective ownership of the religious community is fully expressed in *waqf,* even in cases where one person alone has the management of it. Secondly, the inalienability of the basic property of the *waqf.* Thirdly, collective usage is noticed residually in *waqf,* so that it has the basic purpose of providing for charity, schools, mosques, almshouses, public water supplies and other establishments that would benefit the community - and not for individual usage. And fourthly, *waqf* is frequently concentrated in areas in which the institution of

---

[73] Sayyid MukhtÉr al-BukhÉrÊ and his descendants trace his descent to MÉsÉ al-KÉÐim, the seventh ImÉm; BukhÉrÊ, Langgar, 12 April 2006.

protection operates fully.[74] This seems not different from the English application towards waqf. *According to the* General Report upon the Moslem Trusts and Foundations in Penang, *waqf* was defined as property in which the proprietary right is wholly relinquished and which is consecrated in such a manner to the service of God that it may be to the benefit of man.[75]

Some of the waqfs are difficult to manage due to the fact that the doner specified the waqf property only for his own family access. This type of waqf is classified as family waqf. This imposes restriction on the public to benefit the property and more importantly discourages the influx of public donation. The real question for all waqf including the public waqf is to generate continious resources. Thus, the management board of waqf tend to seek financial assistance from the government especially The States Islamic Religious Councils which become the sole trustee of waqf property in Malaysia.

The main question here is how the waqf property and funds should be sustained. This is because in principle, funds are to be in eradicating social ills. This would certainly decrease the waqf funds and make it more and more dependent on public donation and governmental funds. This issue must be taken into consideration based on three factors. Firstly, waqf itself is for charitable purposes and not for profit making means. Most of the waqfs are basically liabilities such as mosques, religious schools and orphanages. Secondly, costs to manage waqf and its activities continue to climb while identical sources of financial support have become increasingly volatile due to the increase of

---

[74] Mohd. Zain bin Haji Othman, *Islamic Law with Special Reference To The Institution of Waqf,* Kuala Lumpur: (1982), Department of Islamic Affairs, Prime Minister's Department, p. 5.

[75] General Report Upon the Moslem Trusts and Foundations in Penang, *Handbook of The Mohamedan and Hindu Endowments Board,* Penang: (1932), Criterion Press, p. 2.

waqf institutions and other charitable organizations competing for funds from both private donations and government support. Thirdly, the people in need are rising thus making the demand for accountability from donors and others are more challenging than ever.

The only viable solution for this problem is the way of redirecting into more directly innovative and inventive activities. However, this should be done by not denying benefits to humanity. Here the extent to which charitable activities and institutions including waqf should be managed as entrepreneurial entities in order to strengthen their self-reliance. This would make them more contributory institutions of the society in a progressive manner.

Istibdal as Entrepreneurial means

So far, the only means to absorb entrepreneurial mechanism in waqf institution is Istibdal. Istibdal is referred to the exchange of waqf property against another property or money in the same or higher value than the original ones. It means either by substituting, purchasing selling, leasing or any other means in accordance with Islamic rules. In Malaysia, istibdal is practiced only in the case in which the founder of such waqf has consented it in the waqf deed. Istibdal cannot be done even though the waqf property was destroyed or such practice would benefit the waqf property unless it has been permited by the Qadi to be excersised.

Nevertheless, in this respect, istibdal should be regarded as constructive because it embodies certain dynamism if it is practiced in transparent manner. Through this concept, the founder or the management of waqf property are allowed to sell the waqf property in order to suit the market conditions. This can be realized through the waqf land. If a waqf land which happens to be originally at the outskirts of a town ends up being in the middle of it due to urban expansion and its value skyrockets as a result, the founder is enabled to exchange the waqf land for another one, and in the process, can either expand the waqf land, again, at the outskirts by purchasing much more land or enrich his waqf with cash. Furthermore, istibdal assumes great importance if such waqfs is originated from cash endowment. This type of waqf is called cash waqf. In Malaysia, the identical type of this waqf is Amanah Saham Wakaf or Waqf share Trust.

However, the question of whether Istibdal is dynamic and constructive is based on the fact that it must not be misused. Due to the possibility of misuse in this system, it becomes a matter of suspicion to the traditional Islamic Jurists such as schools of Shafiees and Malikis. In this respect, Shafiees is the mostly prevailing school of Islamic law in Malaysia. This makes Istibdal less acceptable in Malaysia and the implementation of Istibdal here is based on enforcement and is only applied to cash waqf. Otherwise, Istibdal is exercised by enforcement when a particular waqf land was subjected to land acquisition by the local government for the public purposes of constructing road.

Nevertheless, Istibdal is increasingly practiced in Malaysia because the Shari'ah jurists and officials tend to adopt the view of Hanafiite School of Thought which allows such practice. One of the instances of the case of Istibdal can be seen from the case of Sentosa Waqf in Alor Setar, Kedah. This Waqf land was founded in 1918. In the 1990s; it was then leased to a housing developer for 99 years. Under this concession, the houses are stipulated as leasehold properties for the said duration for RM 4 Million. RM1 Million were disposed to the descendants of the founder and the rest were used as capital investment with the return revenue is to be distributed to the descendants of the founder.

Conclusion

It can be said that charity and the management of charitable institutions including waqf should not be treated as a passive institutions mechanism although in the society which practice market economy. This is because charity presents benevolent means as a complement to Market Economy which is based on profit making through commercialism. The only way of enhancing the integrity of waqf institution in Malaysia is to adopt entrepreneurial approach in the management of waqf properties and funds. This is to increase the self-reliance of waqf while still receiving donations from private and governmental funds.

However, in the context of waqf, the source of financing those charitable activities and institutions has to be continuously sustained because financial and material sources from zakat and sadaqah can not be absorbed into waqf. This is because waqf is mostly associated with individual or family contribution from their personal wealth and not fully regarded as a public institution.

This creates challenges in the management of waqf property especially mosques, graveyards for the Muslims, and other Islamic religious schools, orphanages under Islamic religious foundation. This is because those waqf institutions are only associated with the Muslims and are highly dependent on voluntary donations from the Muslims. This limitation also shows that the founder and the management board of waqf need to be creative in managing and financing their institutions. The only way to sustain its existence is constant funding and this may require those individuals and groups to adopt entrepreneurial dimension in their course. They also have to explore the dynamic orientation and mechanism in waqf management. This may require them to practice istibdal, Exchanging waqf property against another property or cash.

Here, the concept and the system of Istibdal should be explored in order to create innovative way of generating funds into waqf. Through this system, the waqf properties and institutions as a whole will become sustainable in the long term. Otherwise, the foundation of waqf is only practical due to personal commitment of the founder if he or she is still alive.

THE ROLE OF GRAMEEN BANK IN THE SOCIAL DEVELOPMENT OF BANGLADESH

Md. Sayed Uddin

Introduction

This paper examines the social impact of the mechanisms applied by Grameen Bank to improve the social development of its members. In Bangladesh, measuring the activities of non-government organisations (NGOs) is a good proxy for measuring social developments (Islam M. R. & Morg W.J., 2012). The Grameen Bank is a quasi-government agency in Bangladesh (Buckland Jerry, 1998) often regarded as a community development organisation that provides financial and other services, primarily to women through group-based lending schemes. Its major emphasis is on the use of small credit to promote economic and social development such as eliminating poverty and improving the socio-economic conditions of the rural poor. This paper focuses on Grameen Bank's Sixteenth Decisions social development programme to promote social and financial discipline among the rural poor (Wignaraja P. & Sirivardana S., 2004: 367). The study argues that despite existing initiatives, Grameen Bank could better emphasise rural women's utilisation of healthcare services. Studies have found that women have very limited access to health care services and there was a persisting atmosphere of discrimination in healthcare against females (Pachauri R.K. et al., 2009: 569; Hossen Abul & Westhues Anne, 2011: 1097). In a 2006 report, less than 40 per cent of the population had access to modern primary healthcare services (Pachauri R.K. et al., 2009: 569). This has caused many people to rely on self-treatment when sick, with many visiting a *Kobiraj* (traditional healer). People are only transferred to proper healthcare facilities at a very late stage of the illness (Pachauri R.K. et al., 2009: 569). Poor women in Bangladesh continue to face various sociocultural barriers to access to healthcare service including the *Purdah* whereby a woman's body cannot be seen by unrelated males (Hossen Abul & Westhues Anne, 2011: 1089). Another barrier is the requirement that women first acquire their husband's permission before seeking and obtaining medical treatment (Hossen Abul & Westhues Anne, 2011: 1089). Poverty is another substantial reason preventing women from obtaining medical care. Since Grammen Bank has a great number of women borrowers, a special awareness programme could be useful to reduce the barriers to healthcare services in Bangladesh.

This paper briefly introduces the Grameen Bank including its functions, activities and operations in Bangladesh and internationally. In addition, we addresses previous studies on the impacts of the Grameen Bank in various levels of income, employment, productivity, learning, literacy, and women's economic participations on their household decision-making power. Further, the study discusses its social development activities related to the sixteen decisions. This paper suggests that the Grameen Bank's social development programmes need to focus more on women's access to healthcare services in Bangladesh.

The Grameen Bank: A Review

The Grameen Bank (the name Grameen is derived from the word gram which means 'rural' or 'village') is a reputable non-government organisation (NGO) in Bangladesh founded by the Noble Laureate Muhammad Yunus. The shares of the bank are owned by members with 95 % and 5% is owned by the government of Bangladesh (Zielinski Filip, 2010: 403). The bank is globally familiar for its great contribution toward eradicating poverty and providing micro-credit loans to extremely poor and underprivileged women in Bangladesh and around the world. The Grameen Bank started its journey in 1976 with a small pilot project providing small loans to the poor. In its initial stage, a total of $30 was given to 40 poor people at Jobra, a village near the Chittagong University campus (a public university in Bangladesh). In 1983, it became an independent bank and was recognised as an official financial institution (Bernasek & Stanfield, 1997:359). In 2006, Muhammad Yunus and the Grameen Bank were jointly awarded the Noble Peace Prize. Leading the Grameen Bank, Yunus brilliantly presented the "grameen-credit" or micro-credit model, a poverty eradication model provides small loans to the poor without requiring any collateral. The Grameen Bank differs from conventional banks due to its anti-collateral system of loans. In addition, the Bank's borrowers are poor (among the rural landless), illiterate, and among 95% of the members are women (Hussain Md. M. et al., 2001: 29). Its principles, norms and loan requirements have shown a different mechanism from the conventional bank. Further, its peer monitoring system of micro-credit loan is unique in nature and is based on social collateral (Zielinski Filip, 2010: 403; Hassan M.K. & Renterie-Guerrero L., 1997; Buckland J., 1998: 244), or collective responsibility (Hussain Md. M. et al. 2001: 31).

The social collateral mechanism provides small loans to poor women on the basis of peer groups. A peer group refers to a group comprising five borrowers. From each peer group, one or two borrowers are allowed to receive the loan by rotation. However, the loan repayments' accountability goes to all members in the peer group (Jerry Buckland, 1998). The other borrowers have a chances to receive a loan if the initial loans were properly repaid (Pramanik A.H., 2000). In the self-selection process of members in a peer group, it is important that they are residents of the same village, perhaps the next-door neighbours, and one of the important conditions for peer members is that they must know each other, and one must be liable for the others' loan repayment (Hussain Md. M. et al. 2001: 27).

In addition, the bank has other services of mandatory savings including the individual saving account, group fund and deposits schemes (from the beginning, group members save one Taka per week), which have been used for various purposes. The borrowers can utilise these savings in emergencies such as in cases of illness, ceremonies and other social commitments with 0% interest while most rural development banks have ignored this type of saving services (Hassan M.K. & Renteria-Guerrero L., 1997: 1501). At a glance, the Grameen Bank has provided a wide range of activities such as small loans "(grameen credit)," deposits, housing loans, micro enterprise loans, special programs for beggars, scholarships for the high-performing children of Grameen borrowers (with priority on girls), higher-education loans, loan insurance programs, life insurance for borrowers, pension fund for borrowers, and retirement benefits for bank staff to improve the social and economic conditions (International Encyclopaedia of Civil Society, 2010: 803). With this wide range of lending schemes, savings and deposits programmes and others services, the Grammen Bank had 8,636,951 members (female 8,315,242 and male 321,709), 2,568 branch offices that worked in 81,390 villages as of December 2014 (data source from the Grameen Bank website December 2014: http://www.grameen-info.org/monthly-reports-11-2014/).

The success of the Grameen Bank micro-credit model is its innovative financing mechanism which has been effectively reaching poor families in Bangladesh. Its vital policy is that the its staff go to the rural community rather than people come to the bank

(Pramanik A.H., 2000). Moreover, all sales and support activities are usually performed by the Bank employees in the villages and at the client's homes which can be considered a different attribute from traditional banks (Zielinski Filip, 2010: 403). Grameen Bank staff closely supervise the borrower's social life and business activities with the purpose of supporting them to pay back the loan. This approach has resulted in 98% repayment (Hussain Md. M. et al., 2001: 29), while the conventional bank has a very low percentage of repayment. Its founder Yunus believes that, "credit is a basic human right, and the borrowers are not simply borrowing money from a bank, but are committed to a philosophy build upon four basic principles: disciplines, unity, courage and hard work" (Hussain Md. M. et al., 2001: 29; Zielinski Filip, 2010: 403). This philosophy and close supervision cultivate trust between the Bank, staff and the borrowers through interacting in weekly meetings, while the traditional banks provide loans and wait for the return (Hussain Md. M. et al., 2001: 27).

The Grameen Bank micro-credit model has had a positive impact on women's social and economic conditions in rural Bangladesh. Most importantly, the bank changes the status of women from being marginalised to become independent family and social actors in the community (Rouf K.A., 2012: 285). In Bangladesh, women's social status and economic condition are limited, with limited access and control over household resources (Nasrullah Amir M. & Dickson Keith, 2011: 30). In a patriarchal society like Bangladesh, women are attributed a lower status than men who control households and society, while women are often quiet with heavy domestic workloads, restricted mobility and taking care of children (Hussain Md. M et al. 2001: 30; Nasrullah Amir M. & Dickson Keith, 2011: 30). Rouf (2012) found that this patriarchal society prevents women from being independent actors in the family and community (Rouf K.A., 2012: 285). However, through the Grameen Bank micro-credit scheme, women have shown their potential and hard work that has changed their status in households and created new leadership in the community. By mobilising income generating loans from the bank, women have contributed to family expenses, children education and other matters while their husbands are unable to run family properly. Their involvement in the local government system (the Bangladesh Union Counsel has been a form of local governance) are increasing as they are now elected for chairmanship and councillor positions (Rouf, K.A., 2012). According to Rouf, "the Grameen Bank groups and centre management and leadership development processes have empowered its members to participate more actively in their communities" (Rouf, K.A., 2012: 288).

Moreover, reducing the poverty line among poor households in Bangladesh is another remarkable success of Grameen Bank's micro-credit model. Its micro-credit model and principles have been adopted by many organisations in developing and developed countries. According to a report, the model has been adopted in more than 50 countries across Asia, Europe, Africa, Oceania and in the USA (Hussain Md. M. et al., 2001:26). It was implemented in the United States of America (USA), Canada and Norway to underprivileged low-income female earners, particularly providing small-scale credit to women. For example, in 1986, the Grameen model was introduced in a micro enterprise program called women's self-employment project (WSEP) in Chicago, USA. WSEP has successfully (its loan repayment rate is 93%) created self-employment among single women who have either very low-income or are on welfare (Hussain Md. M. et al., 2001: 32). Another successful micro-credit lending organisation is Women Bank which started from Lofoton (in Norway) and is famous for promoting equal rights between sexes in Norway. Microcredit and savings schemes have introduced a new approach in small-scale rural credit to Papua New Guinea (Fleischer, 1999: 134). In august 1994, Papua New Guinea adopted Grameen Bank's principles in its micro credit organisation called the Lik Lik Dinau Abitore Trust (LLDAT). Fleischer (1999:134) found that the LLDAT Micro-credit and Savings Scheme has thus far been successful in reaching the huge number of rural women and maintaining a higher repayment rate (92%) than all other micro credit schemes in the country. Gradually, the model and its principles have been adopted by Philippines, Chile, Burkina Faso, Indonesia Malawi, Malaysia, Nepal, Nigeria, Pakistan, Peru, Sri Lanka, Bolivia, Vietnam, Paraguay and Papua New Guinea.

Previous Studies on the Grameen Bank

Many studies have been conducted on the impact of Grameen Bank credit on members' socio-economic benefits and society at large. In this part, the paper explores studies on the impact of Grameen Bank on poor women including levels of income, employment, productivity, learning, literacy, and their household decision-making power.

In an empirical study on the impacts of Grameen Bank's micro-credit on the levels of income, employment, and productivity, Iqbal (2002) investigated landless households in rural Bangladesh. Through interviews with a total of 633 households including those involved and not involved in any micro-credit programme, the research draw on a sample of 13 randomly selected *"thanas"* (sub-districts), of which eight sub-districts had Grameen Bank micro-credit programs in operation, and five had none. Three villages in each Thana were randomly selected. The 633 households divided into three subsamples:

- 301 participating target households are poor landless households receiving credit from the Grameen Bank,
- 250 non-participating target households are poor landless households that are not receiving credit from the Grameen Bank or any other source, and
- 82 non-target households are non-poor households not receiving credit from any source.

Iqbal sought to examine the role of credit on the economic welfare of the rural landless poor in Bangladesh. He found that there is a positive relationship between Grameen Bank micro-credit to the poor and their economic wellbeing. The variables of household income included income earned from farming, livestock and fisheries, manufacturing and processing, trade and shop-keeping, transport business, and other non-farm enterprise activities. The study found that the level of household income is higher for the non-target group than the target group. However, among target households, income levels are higher for those that participate in the Grameen Bank programme than those who are non-participant. These findings show that the use of small amounts of credit has a significant and positive impact on the level of household income and credit is the only positive and significant determinant of household income for 301 target households that actually received Grameen Bank micro-loans.

In terms of household employment, Iqbal found that the level of household employment is highest for target households that receive Grameen Bank credit, followed by non-target households, then target households that do not receive Grameen Bank credit. Iqbal pointed out that there is a significant correlation between employment and the number of potential workers in the family who are available and eligible to work. Moreover, the application of small loans does indeed increase the level of household employment, as measured in labour hours. Further, larger amounts of credit have greater impact on household employment or labour use. Households' productivity was measured based on total factor productivity or net household income per operating costs and labour productivity or income per hour of labour. Iqbal found that both measures show the application of small amounts of credit has significantly increases household productivity and that the size of the credit received does not strongly influence household productivity and level of household income. This shows that credit is the only positive and significant determinant of household income and household productivity for the 301 target group those received Grameen Bank micro-loans. However, the level of household employment has shown that size of the credit received effects the level of household employment. The findings suggest that larger amounts of credit have greater impact on household labour use. Finally, Igbal's own evaluation of the impact of Grameen Bank micro-credit is positive, as he found a positive relationship between micro-credit to poor rural households in Bangladesh and their economic wellbeing, which are characterised by higher labour use, higher incomes and greater productivity.

Rahman (1996) sought to determine whether there is a relationship between Grameen Bank participation and women's empowerment by measuring respondents' income generation, decision-making initiative, family planning, food consumption, and literacy skills. A total of 120 women were interviewed from Borongail and Elashin in Manikganj and Tangail districts, two villages in which Grameen Bank branches were located. This study used both the quantitative and qualitative techniques covering a wide range of questions to women borrowers of the Gameen Bank such as household income generation, household decision-making initiative, family planning, food consumption, literacy/education, health awareness, socio-political awareness, and empowerment. In addition, the study uses cross-tabulation between 5-years, 10-years, and non-loanee groups, and includes a total sample of 120 that were divided into four groups:

(1) Those who have been Grameen Bank loanees for ten years,
(2) Those who have been Grameen Bank loanees for five years,
(3) Those who are about to receive their first Grameen Bank loans, and
(4) Those who have never been Grameen Bank loanees.

Rahman pointed out that the 5-year and 10-year loanee groups are better off compared to the non-loanee groups. For example, the 5-year and 10-year loanee groups have a higher level of mobility outside the home than the non-loanee group. His own evaluation of participation in Grameen Bank is associated with higher levels of economic and social empowerment. The variables of decision-making regarding 'use of contraceptives' and 'who uses them' were found to be significant. On the contrary, several variables were insignificant, including decision-making in the household finances, decision-making on mobility, women's numeracy level and keeping of accounts, an interest in children's education, awareness of basic health practices, attitudes regarding children's marriage, inheritance, and political rights.

Mizan (1994) evaluated the impact of the Grameen Bank on women's power and status between the Grameen Bank women group and non-Grameen Bank group. A group of 100 women participants in the Grameen Bank were interviewed from two Dewannagar in Hathazari upazila and Hetalia in Patuakhali upazila, through survey interviews. In comparison, an equal number of non-participants in Grameen Bank were also interviewed from the same villages. Mizan (1994) highlighted the effect of Bangladeshi rural women's work and income (as a resource) on their conjugal decision-making power from a sociological perspective. Women's power is measured along four dimensions (1) household decision making, (2) control over fertility, (3) use of health care by self and other family members and (4) political participation.

Mizan found a significant correlation between the amount of loan and household decision-making, and income from Grameen Bank and the household decision-making. In the household context, the larger loan is expected to give higher financial power and, in turn, provides higher decision-making power (Mizan N. Ainon, 1994: 116). In the case of fertility control, Mizan found that the greater the participation of women in the Grameen Bank loan program, the higher their control over fertility decisions.

The findings of her study demonstrated the significance of the effect of women's work participation and income earning on their input into fertility decisions. Previous studies on the Grameen Bank also reported that borrowers practice family planning in larger numbers than non-borrowers of other rural couples (Islam-Rahman, 1986; Hossain, 1986).

An important assumption was made by Mizan (1994) that the greater the participation of women in Grameen Bank, the greater will be their use of health care services for self and the family. Author has assumed that women gainful economic participation could make a difference in health care or not. According to Mizan, if this does, then Grameen Bank participants are expected to have more frequent medical care when they are sick than non-Grameen Bank participants (Mizan N. Ainon, 1994: 134). Moreover, Mizan found that both Grameen Bank and Non-Grameen Bank respondents overwhelmingly agree that they have some access to health care. Another key point in this study is the political participation as an important dimension of women's decision-making involved their political participation such as in voting (Mizan, 1994). Author hypothesis is that the greater the participation of women in Grameen Bank, the higher will be their participation in voting. Mizan pointed out that even though women's participation in politics in Bangladesh is substantially increasing, their participation is still negligible compared to that of men. However, women's voting participation is higher at the local level elections (Union Council and Upazila) than at the national level (Presidential and Jatiyo Sangshad) elections (Mizan, N. Ainon, 1994: 136).

Khan (1994) examined the impact of the Grameen Bank on how village women, the majority of whom are "illiterate" and unschooled, are induced and socialised into a new way of thinking about themselves and about each other. Khan collected data from the villages Shonalia and Daily Korotia situated in Tangail district which is the nearest urban centre and is closest to the capital Dhaka. This study adopted an ethnographic method through in depth participant-observation and interviews. The researcher also observed informal meetings between the women, workshop sessions, training classes, branch office visits, schools, interactions in socio-cultural domains such as in the home, at religious festivals, marriage negotiation and wedding celebrations, community gatherings, and so on. Khan found that the Grameen Bank creates a unique sense of community through processes such as group organisation, training sessions, and ritualistic performances. He extended his informal session with informants of Grameen bank through open-ended interviews including their life history narratives in an attempt to reconstruct their childhood, schooling experiences, conditions of living, marriage, previous struggles with poverty, and past influences on their lives.

Khan pointed out that those women who participated in the Grameen Bank wree made to understand the administrative paperwork such as the various types of textual materials that villagers come to handle and use including a passbook, fact sheets, various kinds of forms, group membership applications, loan utilization forms, rosters, ledgers, attendance registers, cash memos and vouchers, mortgage declaration documents, land deeds, signboards, and so on. The women themselves are not required to read any of these. The Bank staff do the actual reading and complete the documents for them. Even though the members do not engage in decoding and encoding, they must be able to make sense of this administrative paperwork (Khan, Sharmin Saleha, 1994). Khan pointed to that the Grameen Bank enters this milieu and creates new needs for literacy, such as in keeping track of dates, using calendars, doing documentation, and maintaining records that associate with modern credit systems. It is obligatory for Bank members to know how to sign their names legibly. Khan found that learning how to sign one's name is considered a major accomplishment by many of the villagers. He narrated how for Runa this minimal literacy skill has affected her own self-perception as much as it has her ability to obtain credit from the Bank: (GB member's own speech)

> I can tell that I entered the Grameen Bank and learned how to write. This is of benefit to me inside myself. Why should I have to go to someone else? Going to someone else is bad. If you know how to do it yourself then you are valued for that. Earlier, I would give *tip shoi* (thumb impressions) but now I can sign my name (S. Saleha Khan, 1994:235).

However, Khan found that Grameen Bank does not offer adult literacy classes nor does it claim that universal literacy as one of its objectives (Khan, Sharmin Saleha, 1994: p 230). There is no provision for adults to acquire literacy along with their bank loans. According to Khan, with initiation into bank-generated activities the members, even those classified as "illiterate," engage in different kinds of literacy practices and begin to display a certain facility with print. They are exposed to and make use of written materials to a much greater extent than other non-participating residents in the village, and this occurs with regularity.

The Social Development Programme of the Grameen Bank:

As mentioned earlier, the social development and non-government organisations (NGOs) activities are interlinked in Bangladesh (Islam M. R. & Morg W.J., 2012). The majority of NGOs' agendas and objectives are to reduce poverty, empower the rural population and women, and work at the grassroots level to improve the living conditions of the poor. In Bangladesh, poverty is identified one of the most important problems (Islam M.R. & Morgan W.J., 2011: 371). It is reported that 67% of Bangladeshi's suffer from poverty (Rouf K. A., 2012). Numerous development activities have been lunched to improve the conditions of the people. For example, a reported 2,800 NGOs out of 22,000 voluntary social organisations are involved in development activities in Bangladesh (Moniruzzaman M., 2007:51). The large number of NGOs thrive because of their effectiveness in innovative participatory approaches in the social and economic development process in changing the conditions of rural people (Moniruzzaman M., 2007). Among the key features of NGO activities in Bangladesh. Firstly, the majority of NGOs have focused their activities on alleviating poverty, and target specific groups including women, farmers, fishermen, wood collectors, daily labourers, domestic maids (Ghai, 1984: 17), the unemployed, and those residing in remote areas and the illiterate. Another common feature of NGOs including the Grameen Bank is providing micro-credit loans as income-generation schemes and social services. They mobilise the poor and guide them to empower themselves through participatory approaches (Moniruzzaman M., 2007).

There are many NGOs in Bangladesh. The most reputable NGOs focus on income-generation and social service provision in Bangladesh and include the Bangladesh Rural Advancement Committee (BRAC), the Grameen Bank, and Proshika Manubik Unnyan Kendra (Proshika) (Buckland J., 1998: 239). According to Buckland, the Grameen Bank is the most narrowly focused of these agencies, providing credit within an innovative and effective peers monitoring system (Buckland, J., 1998:239). The Grammen Bank has contributed to mobilising rural women through participating in economic and social business to improve their daily lives (Hassan M. K. and Renteria-Guerrero L., 1997). This has not only improved their economic conditions and living standards but also improved self-esteem and social status (Hassan M. K. and Renteria-Guerrero L., 1997). Buckland (1998) has rightly stated that NGOs in Bangladesh have set up innovative development models that have improved participant livelihood through efforts in income-generation, social-service provision, and group capacity building (Buckland, Jerry, 1998: 239).

Focusing on the Grameen Bank's social development programmes, from its inception the Grameen Bank had the agenda to alleviate poverty through small loans to the poor. Soon after, the Grameen bank and its originators found borrowers faced difficulties to maintain the financial accounts including lacking knowledge of dealing with technical information and managing the small business properly (Hassan M. K. and Renteria-Guerrero L., 1997). Its majority borrowers are poor illiterate women. Studies on women's empowerment have shown that women's empowerment means social and economic development. Economic growth alone cannot liberate from the male-dominated families (Rouf. K.A., 2012). In 1984, the Grameen Bank established its social development programme called the "Sixteen Decisions" (Rouf. K.A., 2012); a welfare programme for poor people to make more productive. That is what Hussain et al. called Grameen Social Values known as "the Sixteenth Decisions" where members have to improve living standards (Hussain et al., 2001:26). These 16 decisions have become the social development constitution of the Grameen Bank. It has become the focus for the participatory process whenever members meet. Under the "sixteen decisions" members are forced to improve houses, produce foods domestically, eliminate dowry in marriage and keep a healthy environment (Hassan M. K. & Renteria-Guerrero L., 1997).

As Hussain noted, the Grameen Bank has set a condition (one of the 16 decisions) to improve the literacy rate through its book keeping processes and other social agenda (Hussain Md. M., Maskooki K., & Gunasekaran, 2001). Achieving the goal of social development agendas incorporated in "sixteen decisions", the Grameen Bank has been gradually extended special loan programmes such as housing, small loans for installation of hand pumps (for irrigation and drinking water), small loans for building sanitary latrines and seasonal loans for crop production to its members (Rebecca Fleischer, 1999). Fleischer (1999) found that housing loans and other special loans increase borrowers' productive capacity, and provide space for self-employment. The sixteen decisions has raised awareness in various social and women empowerment issues such as organising for dowry-less marriage, anti-teenage marriage, collectively solving neighbour's problems, sinking tube wells for pure drinking water, family planning, education, public health, encourages borrowers to establish schools, pre-schools and day-care services to tutor members' children while they are engaged in their business activities (Rouf K.A., 2012; Hassan M. K. & Renteria-Guerrero L., 1997). Rouf pointed out that the Bank has initiated additional socio-economic, cultural, environmental, health, agricultural and educational programmes to support women's empowerment (Rouf K.A., 2012). The sixteen decisions is the social messages that have been incorporated all social and economic wellbeing matters and discussed in weekly meetings, and delivered social loans, organising various events to achieve the social and economic goal (Joshi, Deepali Pant, 2006: 134).

Moreover, the sixteen decisions emphasises on social intervention in gardening and family planning issues. Members are encouraged to plant trees and grow kitchen gardens, because the development of kitchen gardens often provides a regular income from which the borrower can partly finance the weekly loan instalments (Hassan & Renteria-Guerrero (1997). In addition, its social interventions mostly during the weekly meeting discussion have raised awareness among the poor women to fight against social injustice.

Its family planning agenda is an effective social messages of the sixteen decisions promoted to keep small families among its members. In a study, Mahmud investigated a total of 100 currently married women from four NGOs including the Grameen Bank income-generation programs in Bangladesh (Mahmud, 1994).

Mahmud found that the Grammen Bank and BRAC educated beneficiaries' women have benefited from small families. However, study found that the Grameen Bank annual report has portrayed community poverty alleviation over social development performance. Based on nine years of annual reports, Islam and Mathews (2009) investigated the social performances disclosers' report of the Grameen Bank. The authors selected five major issues relevant to social performance report included in the Millennium Development Goals (MDGs) indicators. These are (1) community poverty alleviation; (2) community health; (3) community education; (4) environmental sustainability; and (5) others. Islam and Mathews found that the poverty alleviation disclosures became the most important part (81 per cent of total social disclosure sentences) of GB's annual report and accounted for the highest proportion of total disclosures while the issue of community health, community education, environmental sustainability and others recorded a low level of disclosure (altogether 19 per cent of total disclosures).

Raising Awareness of Social Welfare Issues: Women's Utilisation of Healthcare Services

Sociologist Midgley (1995:13) considered social development as an approach for promoting social welfare (or social wellbeing). He stated that social welfare is the centre of social development. It exists when families, communities and societies experience a high degree of social wellbeing. Midgley defined social development as, "a process of planned social change designed to promote the well-being of the population as a whole in conjunction with a dynamic process of economic development (1995:25)." Pillai and Maleku (2015) rightly coded from other two texts (Beverly & Sherraden, 1997; United Nations, 1969) that social development is a process of improving the capacity of social systems, social structure institutions to enhance the standard of living and quality of life through accepted social values of individuals and communities (Pillai and Maleku, 2015: 844). They pointed out that in order to build capacity at the individual and community levels, social development programmes focus on healthcare issues. Thus, taking consideration from these definitions of social development, healthcare issues should be addressed in comprehensive for sustainable social and economic development of the community.

In Bangladesh, NGOs have been providing services in three categories including (a) income-generation programmes, e.g. peer-monitored credit; (b) provision of social services, e.g. primary education; and (c) social organising, e.g. establishment of small homogeneous groups for joint savings or peer monitoring of credit (Buckland J., 1998:238). The Grameen Bank is the most narrowly focused that provides credit within an innovative and effective peer monitoring system (Buchland, J., 1998:239). This paper argues that the Grameen Bank should consider and raise awareness campaigns on non-economic benefits of the social welfare programme like utilisation of healthcare services on women in Bangladesh.

In Bangladesh, women have limited access to healthcare services and other resources (Ahmed S.M. et al., 2000; Rouf, 2012). According to the healthcare behaviour model by Andersen (1995), the more resources one has, the more he/she has better access to healthcare services. Rouf pointed out that poor Bangladeshi women lack access to basic human rights like shelter, health, food, clothing, education, and other social needs, and they have been marginalised socially, economically and politically for generations (2012: 286). In an Islamic country like Bangladesh, women have been treated poorly due to the socio-structural patterns of a patriarchal society, especially in rural areas. Women have limited scope in household decision-making, while husbands' involvement in decision-making is particularly important in Bangladesh because men often dominate household decisions related to large health-related purchases (Story WT &

Burgard SA., 2012). In addition, Ahmed and his associates (2000) pointed to the existing socio-economic differentials between the health status of the wealthy few and the great number of the poor, due to inequalities in education, healthcare access and ability to pay (Ahmed S.M. et al., 2000). Evidently, food and healthcare are disproportionately distributed to male children in Bangladesh, and infant and child mortality rates are higher among girls. Ahmed and his colleagues found that females are significantly less likely to seek care than males in both households those are member of BRAC (a reputed NGO) and poor non-member households (Ahmed et al., 2000). Moreover, their results have shown that sick (woman) individual of BRAC member households tendsto seek care less frequently than non-members. Surprisingly, authors have pointed out that both BRAC members and non-member groups, women suffering illnesses report seeking care significantly less often than men. In addition, BRAC members depend on home remedies, traditional care, and unqualified allopath than non-member households. Amin et al. (2001) found similar results in a study among micro-credit programs for women (Amin Ruhul et al., 2001). Amin and his associates found that uses of traditional health providers such as village healers, homeopaths, or herbalists (*Kabiraj/ Hakims)* were equally used in both the remote and urban areas. Similarly, a study has conducted in two non-government agencies in rural and town based settings, found that a woman borrower decided to seek solutions for her sick son from the religious teachers used *pani pora, tel pora* (blessed water, blessed oil) from a *huzur* (religious teacher) to cure her son in order to save the little money she had (Moniruzzaman M., 2007:41).

Thus, the socio-structural pattern and economic barriers to women limit their use and access to healthcare facilities in Bangladesh. In addition, the majority of studies found that women borrowers have a tendency to use healthcare providers such as from traditional healers and religious teachers in order to save the little money they had. However, it is also evident that participation in a credit programme has a positive impact on a woman's decision to seek formal healthcare (Nanda P., 1999). In sixteen decisions, one of the rule is "We intend to have small families. We shall reduce our expenses to a minimum. We take care of our health." This decision or social message shows a combination of three awareness messages, including fertility control, encourage keep savings, and taking care of health in general. This paper suggests that for the betterment of the poor women's access to healthcare services, the Grameen Bank could promote additional social awareness campaigns to help reduce the barriers in utilising healthcare facilities in Bangladesh.

Critical issues in the Grameen Bank:

The Grameen Bank has not gone without criticism. It has never forgiven a loan, not even after a flood, or a cyclone (Hussain et al., 2001:32). A very common criticism about Grameen is its higher interest rates reaching 20 percent whereas the conventional banking charged at 10-15 percent (Hussain et al. 2001:32). Another, is its social development constitution the "sixteen decisions" related awareness campaigns, seminar, workshops which have been discontinued and the rules (16 decisions) are just in the borrowers' passbooks which they listen to only during weekly meetings (Rouf. K.A., 2012). In addition, the social issue of dowry and the male power attitude of patriarchal power still exist in rural families and community (Rouf. K.A., 2012). Researchers also claim that women's larger mobility and visibility often lead to increased exposure to violence. For instance, women's increased role in decision making may cause men to take less responsibility and withdrew support for critical decisions like healthcare seeking (Simeen & Nirali, 2012). However, the Grameen Bank has accomplished a great deal, designing a mechanism of micro-finance model to drive efficient performance, reaching poor borrowers, and inspiring a movement in micro-lending for improving the living conditions of rural women in Bangladesh.

Conclusions:

Despite its critics, the Grameen Bank micro-credit is an effective tool to eradicate poverty among the poor in Bangladesh. It has demonstrated that the poor are bankable and are capable of making good business. It has created huge self-employment and income generation schemes primarily for women. It further improved the quality of housing, increased their family income, kept families small, educated children, and eschewed dowry. The sixteen decisions programmes of social development have raised consciousness about primary healthcare, nutrition, maternal and child care, family planning, sanitation, plantation and vegetable growing (Hassan M.K. & Renteria-Guerrero L., 1997; Rouf K.A., 2012; Fleischer R., 1999; Rahman, 1986). It is evident that the Grameen Bank has covered many serious social welfare issues through the sixteen decisions including healthcare. However, this paper claims that it should consider programmes and raise awareness on women's healthcare utilisation in Bangladesh. The Bank could take rigorous initiatives to encourage women's easy access to healthcare facilities. Women's access to healthcare services is at a low among poor women in Bangladesh. They have limited access in resources including health services. Therefore, the Grameen Bank could take new initiatives and disseminate the message to women borrowers emphasising the utilisation of healthcare services through a series of programmes, weekly meetings, workshops, seminars and conferences.

REFERENCES

Ahmed, Mahbub. (1985). *Status, Perception, awareness and Marital Adjustment of Rural Women.* Grameen Bank.

Ahmed Syed Masud, Alayne M. Adams b, Mushtaque Chowdhurya, Abbas Bhuiyac. (2000). Gender, socioeconomic development and health-seeking behaviour in Bangladesh. *Social Science & Medicine,* 51 (3), 361-371.

Andersen Ronald M. (1995). Revisiting the Behavioral Model and Access to Medical Care: Does it Matter? *Journal of Health and Social Behavior,* Vol. 36, No. 1, 1-10.

Amin Ruhul, Maurice st. Pierre, Ashraf Ahmed & Runa Haq. (2001). Integration of an essential services package (ESP) in child and reproductive health and family planning with a micro-credit program for poor women: Experience from a pilot project in rural Bangladesh. *World Development, vol. 29, no. 9, 1611-1621.*

Buckland, Jerry. (1998). Social capital and sustainability of NGO intermediated development projects in Bangladesh. *Community Development Journal,* vol. 33 No. (3), 236-248.

Beverly, S.G. & Sherraden,M.(1997)'Investment in human development as a social development strategy'. *Social Development Issues,* 19, pp. 1–18.

Bernasek, A. & Stanfield, James, Ronald. (1997). The Grameen bank as progressive institutional adjustment. *Journal of Economic Issue, Vol. 31* (2), 359-366.

Fleischer Rebecca. (1999). "Replicating Grameen in Papua New Guinea", *Humanomics,* Vol. 15 (2), pp. 110 – 144.

Ghai, Dharam. (1984). *An evaluation of the impact of the Grameen Bank project.* Dhaka: Grameen Bank.

Hassan M. Kabir & Renteria-Guerrero Luis. (1997), "The experience of the Grameen Bank of Bangladesh in community development", *International Journal of Social Economics,* Vol. 24 (12) pp. 1488-1523.

Hossen, Abul & Westhues Anne. (2011). Improving Access to Government Health Care in Rural Bangladesh: The Voice of Older Adult Women. *Health Care for Women International*, 32:1088–1110.

Hussain Md. Mostaque, Kooros Maskooki & A. Gunasekaran. (2001). "Implications of Grameen banking system in Europe: prospects and prosperity". *European Business Review,* Vol. 13 Iss 1 pp. 26-42.

Islam, Muhammad Azizul & Mathews, Martin Reginald. (2009). "Grameen Bank's social performance disclosure". *Asian Review of Accounting*, vol. 17 (2) pp. 149 -162.

Islam M. R. & Morg W. J., (2012). Non-governmental organizations in Bangladesh: their contribution to social capital development and community empowerment. *Community Dev J*, 47 (3): 369-385.

Iqbal, Jhilam Zebunnessa. (2002). The impact of Grameen Bank credit on the levels of income, employment, and productivity of poor landless households in rural Bangladesh. New York: Fordham University.

Joshi Deepal Pant (2006). Social Banking: Promise, performance and potential. Foundation Book Pvt. Ltd. Cambridge House: New Delhi.

Khan, Sharmin Saleha, (1994). Banking on women: Learning, literacy and human development in the Grameen Bank, Bangladesh. Berkeley: University of California.

Mahmud, S. (1994). The role of women's employment programmes in influencing fertility regulation in rural Bangladesh. *Bangladesh Development Studies,* 22 (2-3), pp. 93-119.

Midgley, James. (1995). *Social development: The developmental perspective in social welfare.* London: Eng. Sage.

Mizan, <u>Ainon Nahar</u>. (1994). In quest of empowerment the Grameen Bank impact on women's power and status, Dhaka: The University Press Limited.

Moniruzzaman M. (2007): Group Formation and Empowerment: The Case of Brac and Proshika in Bangladesh. *Intellectual Discourse,* vol, 15, No. 1, 37-58.

<u>Nanda P.</u> (1999). Women's participation in rural credit programmes in Bangladesh and their demand for formal health care: is there a positive impact? <u>*Health Econ.*</u> Vol. 8(5):415-28.

Nasrullah Amir M. & Dickson Keith (2011). *Empowerment of rural women, decent employment and micro enterprise development programs of NGOs in Bangladesh. International Journal of Afro-Asian Studies,* vol. 2, No. 2, 30-40.

Rahman, Ruba. (1996). *An empirical analysis of the relationship between Grameen Bank participation and women's empowerment.* USA: Michigan State University.

<u>Pachauri</u> R. K., <u>Luc Gnacadja</u>, <u>Hans Günter AFES-PRESS, Michael Zammit Cutajar, Achim Steiner, Navnita Chadha Behera, Sàlvano Briceno, Patricia Kameri-Mbote, Joy Ogwu,Stavros Dimas, Vandana Shiva, John Grin, Úrsula Oswald Spring, Béchir Chourou, Czeslaw Mesjasz, Heinz Krummenacher.</u> (2009). *Facing Global Environmental Change: Environmental, Human, Energy, Food, Health and Water Security Concepts.* Springer Science & Business Media.

Pramanik Ataul Huq. (2000). "Whither Welfare States? The Lessons from Fast-Growing East Asian Emerging Economies and the Grameen Bank Model". *Humanomics, Vol.* 16 Iss 2 pp. 3 – 18.

Pillai Vijayan K. & Maleku Arati. (2015). Reproductive Health and Social Development in Developing Countries: Changes and Interrelationships. *British Journal of Social Work,* 45, 842–860.

Rouf, Kazi Abdur. (2012). "A feminist interpretation of Grameen Bank Sixteen Decisions campaign". *Humanomics,* Vol. 28 Iss 4 pp. 285 – 296.

Simeen Mahmud & Nirali M. Shah (2012). Measurement of women's empowerment in rural Bangladesh. *World development,* vol. 40 (3), pp. 610-619.

Story WT, & Burgard SA. (2012). Couples' reports of household decision-making and the utilization of maternal health services in Bangladesh. *Soc Sci Med.* 75(12):2403-11.

United Nations (1969) The Role of Social factors in Development (Expert Group Meeting on Social Policy and Planning, Background Paper No. 2), Stockholm, United Nations.

Wignaraja Ponna & Sirivardana Susil (Eds.). (2004). Pro-poor growth and governance in south Asia: Decentralization and participatory development. India: Sage Publications India Pvt. Ltd.

Yunus, M. (1987). *Credit for self-employment: A fundamental human right.* Dhaka: The Grameen Bank.

Yunus, M. (1989). *Strategy for the decade of the nineties.* Dhaka: The Grameen Bank.

Yunus, Muhammad. (1982). Grameen Bank in Bangladesh-A Poverty Focused Rural Development Program." Grameen Bank Publication Series No. 19, p.6.

Zielinski Filip (2010). Grameen Bank. In Helmut K. Anheier, Stefan Toepler (Eds.), International Encyclopedia of Civil Society 2010. pp.803-804. Springer.

END NOTES

1. Apter, David E., *Rethinking Development* (London, New Delhi: Sage Publications, 1987).
2. Esteva, G., Development in Sachs, W. (ed.) *The Development Dictionary: A guide to Knowledge as Power* (Johannesburg: Witwatersrand University Press, 1992).
3. Willis, K., *Theories and Practices of Development* (Abingdon, Oxon: Routledge, 2005).
4. Apter, David E., *Rethinking Development*, 7.
5. Rose, G., *Deciphering Sociological Research* (Basingstoke: Macmillan, 1982).
6. GNP is the value of the economic output resulting from the use of resources – labour, land, capital owned by national members of the society.
7. Barnett, Tony, *Social And Economic Development: An Introduction* (New York and London: The Guilford Press, 1989), 180.
8. GDP per head is calculated by dividing the total value of economic activity by the total population.
9. Morris, M. D., *Measuring the conditions of the World's Poor* (New York: Pergamon Press 1979).
10. Coleman, James S., "The Development Syndrome: Differentiation – Equality – Capacity" in Beinder, L. (ed.) *Crisis and Sequence in Political Development* (Princeton: Princeton University Press, 1974), 75 – 76.

11. Ibid., 74.

12. Mukherjee Ramkrishna, *Society Culture Development* (New Delhi/Newbury Park/ London: Sage Publications, 1991), 11.

13. Ibid., 13.

14. Barnett Tony, *Social And Economic Development: An Introduction*, 14.

15. Braudel, Fernand, *The Structure of Everyday Life* (London: William Collins and Sons, 1981), 557.

16. Spencer, Herbert, *The Evolution of Society* (Chicago: University of Chicago Press, 1967), 3-5.

17. Barnett, Tony, *Social and Economic Development: An Introduction*, 19.

18. Ibid., 21.

19. Weber, Max, *The Protestant Ethic and the Spirit of Capitalism* (London:Unwin 1967).

20. Ritzer, George, *Contemporary Sociological Theory and Its Classical Roots* (Boston Burr Ridge: Mc Graw Hill, 2003), 27.

21. Kiely Ray, *Sociology and Development: The Impasse and Beyond* (London: VCL Press Ltd. University College, London, 1955), 35 with reference to Thomas, A, Third world: images, definition, connotations in Open University U204, *Third World Studies*, Block 1, 1-45. and Worsley, P., *The third world* (London: Weidenfeld & Nicholson, 1964).

22. Ibid., 37.

23. Ibid.

24. Moore, W. E., *Social Change* (New Jersey: Prentice Hall, 1964), 89.

25. McClelland, David, *The Achieving Society* (New York: Free Press. 1961).

26. Rostow, Walt, *The Stages of Economic Growth* (Cambridge: Cambridge University Press,1960), 4 – 16.

27. Ibid., 17 – 35.

28. Moore, W., *The Impact of Industry* (New Jersey: Prentice-Hall, 1965),10; Rostow, Walt, *The Stages of Economic Growth*, 180.

29. Kerr et al., *Industrialism and Industrial Man* (London: Heinemann,1962), Chs. 1 &2

30. Moore, W., The Impact of Industry 1965, 11-12.

31. Gallie, D., *Social Inequality and Class Radicalism in France and Brtiain* (Cambridge: Cambridge University Press, 1983).

32. Barnett Tony, *Social and Economic Development: An Introduction* 36.

33. Kiely Ray, *Sociology and Development: The Impasse and Beyond*, 39.

34. Lenin, Vladimir, Selected Works (Moscow: Progress,1977), 248.

35. Stalin, J. V., *Problems of Leninism* (Peking: Foreign Language Press,1976), 859.

36. Frank, A. G., *Capitalism and Underdevelopment in Latin America* (Harmonds- worth: Penguin, 1971), 27.

37. Baran, Paul, *The Political Economy of Growth* ((New York: Monthly Review Press,1957), 141 – 2.

38. Ibid., 22 – 4.

39. Wallerstein Immanuel, *The Modern World System: Capitalist Agriculture and the Origin of the European World Economy in the Sixteenth Century* (New York: Academic Press, 1974), 7.

40. Emmanuel Arghiri, *Unequal Exchange* (London: New Left Books,1972), 42.

41. Ibid., 43.

42. Quoted by Keily with reference to Amin, S., *Unequal Development* (Hassocks: Harvester, 1966), 288.

43. Keily, Ray, *Sociology and Development: The Impasse and Beyond*, 47.

44. Ibid., 57.

45. Gulalp, H., Debate on Capitalism and Development: the Theories of Samir Amin and Bill Warren, *Capital and Class* 28, 135-59. 1986:155

46. Keily, Ray, *Sociology and Development: The Impasse and Beyond*, 58.

47. Ansari Mohammad I, "Islamic Perspectives on Sustainable Development", *The American Journal of Islamic Social Sciences*, Vol. 11, Fall 1994, No. 3, pp. 394. He also referred to: Easterlin, R. A. "Does Economic Growth Improve Human Lot? Some Empirical Evidence." *In Nations and Households in Economic Growth*, edited by P. A. David and M. W. Reder (New York: Academic Press, 1974). Scitovsky, Tibor, "Two Concepts of External Economies," *The Journal of Political Economy*, No.17, 1954, 143 – 51. ....*Papers on Welfare and Growth* (Stanford, CA: Stanford University Press, 1964). ....*The Joyless Economy* (New York: Oxford University Press, 1976).

48. Qur'an, 13: 11.

49. Qur'an, 8: 53.

50. Qur'an, 24: 55.

51. Qur'an, 10: 13.

52. Ahmad, Khurshid, "Islamic Approach to Development", in Zeenath Kausar ed. *Political Development: An Islamic Approach* (Kuala Lumpur: The Other Press and International Islamic University, Malaysia, 2000), 19.

Printed in the United States
By Bookmasters